MOON SHOT

MOON SHOT

THE ULTIMATE GUIDE TO OUTRAGEOUS
NETWORK MARKETING SUCCESS

SANDRO CAZZATO

LIONCREST
PUBLISHING

MOON SHOT
The Ultimate Guide to Outrageous Network Marketing Success

FIRST EDITION

ISBN 978-1-5445-5039-8 *Hardcover*
     978-1-5445-5038-1 *Paperback*
     978-1-5445-5040-4 *Ebook*
     978-1-5445-5041-1 *Audiobook*

To my tribe, who has been with me from the beginning,
and the leaders I've met along the way.

CONTENTS

Network Marketing can give you
everything, if you want everything!

FOREWORD

—ERIC WORRE, AUTHOR OF *GO PRO: 7 STEPS TO BECOMING A NETWORK MARKETING PROFESSIONAL*

Every profession needs new voices. It's a sign of health and vitality that new blood enters the business with their own ideas about how to do things. Network marketing is no different. We need people to rise up and provide fresh energy and perspectives.

So I take it as proof of network marketing's maturity that we have people like Sandro in this space today, making it his own.

I was impressed by Sandro from the start. I first met him in December 2022 at a Go Pro event, part of my Network Marketing Pro program where I try to raise the level of professionalism in network marketing and improve the results for individual leaders. I've been working as a network marketing coach for decades now—and I've been in the business even longer. I've sat down with those at the top of our profession and met thousands upon thousands of earnest, hardworking network marketers climbing their way toward the top.

Sandro, I can confidently say, is among the most accomplished people in network marketing I've ever met. Elegant, professional, and quietly confident, I could immediately feel this undercurrent of positive intent in everything he put his mind to. At that moment, he was putting his mind to network marketing, and he was already achieving remarkable results.

As Sandro recognizes in this book, the key to his success has been a recognition that network marketing is more than a "get rich quick" scheme—it's a profession. I've dedicated my career to convincing people to "go pro" in network marketing and see it as a professional calling akin to entrepreneurship. Sandro had clearly already arrived at the same point.

And because he recognized it as a serious business, he was an eager student.

I've had thousands of "students" of network marketing attend my events and read my books. But only a handful of them ever really listen to what I've been trying to say and fully implement the ideas. So many pretend to listen. They take notes; they nod along. Then they toss everything aside and do things the way they wanted to from the beginning.

Sandro is different. He's a voracious student who truly listens and absorbs ideas like a sponge. He's ready to investigate and experiment with any new strategy. When it works, he implements it into his own process.

That's really just the beginning of what Sandro brings to network marketing. His drive, focus, and consistency are truly impressive. He's relentless in his efforts to grow his own business, help others build theirs, and spread the word about network marketing's potential to those who don't know all it has to offer.

Above all else, Sandro is a team player. I've never seen someone so committed to his team. He's always pushing himself and everyone else forward. He's a constant guide to people across his organization—from those who signed with him on day one to those who just entered yesterday.

And he never slows down. No matter how successful he gets, he just keeps going.

For all those reasons, I wasn't surprised when Sandro told me he was writing this book. He's a systematic thinker, on top of everything else, and I knew he'd bring together a structured framework that anyone with ambition and drive could follow to network marketing success.

Sandro is as honest as he is focused, and he's laid out his entire system for you here. He's followed every step himself, and he's watched thousands of others follow them after him. He offers a well-devised system that's been tested and proven thousands of times. And on top of it all, this book is a really enjoyable read.

Like me, Sandro dreams of showing the world the potential within network marketing. This book is a fantastic introduction to the core concepts of the business model and the steps you can follow to transform your life.

So my advice to you, Reader, is to channel your inner Sandro when reading this book. Pay close attention. Highlight key ideas. Take notes. Really let it sink in.

Then get to work.

Ahead, when Sandro details the potential of network marketing, just know that he isn't exaggerating. In a matter of months, you can be working for yourself in a business you've built by your own efforts, making more than you ever have before.

That's how I did it. It's how Sandro did it. And he and I have both seen it work thousands of times before.

To see truly incredible results, though—to "walk on the moon," as Sandro would say—you need the advice in this book.

Pay attention. It may just change your life.

INTRODUCTION

People keep asking me how I did it.

How did I create one of the most successful network marketing businesses in the whole profession in just four years? How do I stay motivated and keep growing the business every day? And how am I going to justify sharing all my secrets in one book?

To answer these questions, we have to go back to the moment I took the leap into network marketing. It was 2020, and I seemed to have everything. I was thirty-six years old with a lovely, loving wife and great kids. I ran my own IT consulting company that offered services to Swiss banks and insurance companies. For many, this would be a dream job. I had plenty of money in my bank account, and my job mostly focused on facilitating connections between the IT experts at my company and influential people in the banking sector who needed their services. That meant I spent my evenings eating at Michelin star restaurants and my weekends at five-star hotels with some of the wealthiest people in Switzerland.

What a life, right?

But I was completely unsatisfied. I had everything, and I wasn't happy. Worse, I had no right to complain! I was successful and well off. No one wants to hear about how someone in my position is miserable. But I couldn't chase away this feeling of emptiness. I had no vision, no motivation, and no passion. I had to force myself to go into work each day. I came home exhausted and grouchy.

I even began to question the other parts of my life that seemed so perfect. Was there something wrong with my marriage? I loved my kids, but had I become a father too early? I couldn't shake the feeling that life was passing me by. I was on a runaway train, and the brake was broken.

I hate to think what would have happened if I hadn't stumbled upon network marketing. Luckily, I stumbled upon the work of the network marketing master Eric Worre online one day. I bought his book and read it in forty-eight hours. Then I participated virtually in his annual big event "Go Pro."

I couldn't get enough. Suddenly, everything clicked into place. I saw a career path that opened up incredible potential, doing work I found interesting and invigorating. I was so grateful to find that opportunity. I put everything into it—and in the process grew one of the largest network marketing businesses on the planet.

Today, I have a team of thousands. I've helped make six people millionaires. Several hundred more now make six figures a year. Thousands of others are making more than they ever did in their previous careers, each one of them now running their own business.

This book is about how I did it—and the process I developed that helped all those other people do the same.

Using this system, each of us aimed for the moon, built our own rocket ship, launched it, and successfully landed there. All in the matter of a few years. Together, we've been the NASA of network marketing. And we're looking for new astronauts eager to take the next flight.

DO YOU WANT TO DO BETTER THAN OKAY?

Before you go any further, I have to warn you: *if you follow the advice of this book, you risk becoming a millionaire.*

I know that sounds like a very bold claim, and maybe you're a little wary of it because you've heard so many others promise you the sky and let you down. But I'm making that claim out of experience—and not just my own. I've developed a step-by-step process to get a company up, running, and flying in network marketing, and I've seen a number of people reach that seven-figure dream. Hundreds are making hundreds of thousands of dollars off this system, and thousands are making more than they ever did in their previous career.

So you're right to be skeptical when people make such big promises, but I believe I can back this one up. And I'm going to spend the rest of the book proving it to you.

Network marketing, for those of you who don't know, is a business model in which individuals build their own businesses by selling products or services from a supplier to the people in their social network. At the same time, they then recruit others who will sell to their connections and recruit in their own right.

This business model has been around for decades, and it brings in more than two hundred billion dollars of revenue each year. But up until now, it has been difficult to find a strategy that really opens up the true potential for success inherent in the model.

True, there are books that lay out the basic principles for success in this field—but we're looking for outrageous success. That's why I have developed my step-by-step guide that lays out what it takes to shoot for the moon from day one to day 121. This book shows you how to grow a business every day from the moment you sign up to the moment you step foot on the moon as yet another network marketing massive success story.

The strategy I'm going to lay out in this book has delivered almost unbelievable results. And it's done so over and over again. The key difference between this strategy and others you will encounter in this space is that I have recognized that almost everyone has been wrong about network marketing. Network marketing isn't a scam. And it isn't a get-rich-quick-for-almost-no-effort-and-then-get-out opportunity either. ***It's a way into entrepreneurship that costs less and takes less time than starting your own business the traditional way.***

In traditional business, you have to invest thousands of dollars in rent, products, marketing, and staff. Often, you have to take out costly loans or go to business school or learn to code. Traditional entrepreneurship is great for those who have a product in mind and have the ability and desire to invest heavily in getting it off the ground. But so many people want to be entrepreneurs but lack the ability for one reason or another. That's where network marketing fills a huge gap. None of those investments is necessary in network marketing. You don't need to take a risk opening a restaurant or an outlet store. You don't have to figure out payroll or even come up with your own product. That's all taken care of for you. You can jump into business today and earn income while you learn the business by doing it.

At the same time, network marketing isn't a secret way you can earn passive/residual income with hardly any effort. You may earn some of that income down the line, but your main job in network marketing is *building a business that lasts*—and then maintaining it. If you're willing to sweat for this, you can scale your business faster than entrepreneurs in any other profession.

In other words, network marketing offers you a way into entrepreneurship for less money and can lead to success in less time. But you still have to work as hard as the entrepreneurs who do open those businesses. Network marketing can transform your life, but it requires passion, dedication, and sacrifice.

With network marketing, you really can start anywhere on Earth, build your rocket, and reach the moon. But to do so, you have to be willing to throw yourself into the process. If you do, network marketing can pay you back better than any business investment out there.

AN EXTRA SEAT ON THE NEXT ROCKET SHIP

My speech in Frankfurt was about responsibility. If you enter network marketing, your aim is always to build your own business. Once you commit to that goal, you have to realize you're signing up not just for potential wealth but real responsibility. You become the captain of your own rocket ship, and a captain's responsibility is to take care of their crew.

In my speech, I highlighted one captain who failed his responsibilities: Captain Schettino. He was the Italian captain of a ship that capsized after striking underwater rocks off the coast of the island of Giglio in Italy. Instead of staying with the ship and helping his passengers and crew, he fled, saving himself while dozens died.

We live in a society these days that encourages that kind of selfish leadership—get rich quick and get out before anyone notices you took advantage of them. I don't support that kind of thinking. And that's why I love network marketing. The key to success in this profession isn't getting rich quick; it's supporting everyone you bring into the business, *lifting them up with you*. Those are the qualities of a good captain.

The paycheck is nice. The acclaim is nice. But it isn't all one-sided. People will look up to you, and you have to be there for them. They'll come to you with their questions and problems starting their own businesses, and you have to be there to help.

I feel this responsibility deeply. In fact, that's why I'm writing this book. I want to extend my responsibility beyond my team and offer every one of you a seat on the next network marketing rocket before it blasts off.

And I want you to build that rocket for yourself. I've done very well in my business. In fact, I could retire today and continue to make income for the rest of my life at this point. I don't need or want anything from you. I simply believe in the potential of this profession, and I want to share that potential with others.

There's no gimmicks here, no tricks. You don't have to buy anything from me or send me a cent. This is about legacy for me. It's a chance to improve lives. All I ask is that you give me a chance to show you how it's done, and if you believe in the vision, commit to it yourself.

THE PROFESSION OF THE TWENTY-FIRST CENTURY

One of the main reasons I'm so passionate about sharing the ideas in this book is because I fervently believe we are entering the era of network marketing. This business model has so many advantages over the other ways of doing business that it is poised to become one of the most significant ways we do commerce for the rest of the twenty-first century.

This isn't just a hunch. There are many compelling reasons to believe network marketing represents the future. In the first place, workers have a new perspective on work. Before COVID-19, most people expected to find a job, go into an office or worksite, and put in forty or more hours a week for a paycheck. But COVID-19 proved work could be different for many of us. We could work from home, set our own schedules, and work on projects at our own pace. This new setup made many of us more productive—and made us realize just how miserable we were in the old system. Now that businesses are clawing back many of those benefits, people can see there should be a better way to do things.

Network marketing offers that better way. You can work from home or anywhere. You work for yourself, setting your hours, your workload, and your responsibilities. Instead of working away your whole life in a cubicle or behind a counter, dreaming of a few weeks of vacation each year at best, you can work on a beach for the rest of your life and make more money while doing it!

A profession that's more flexible, more lucrative, and allows for maximum independence? That sounds like a twenty-first century career to me.

But that's not the only reason to believe in network marketing. It offers more than money and independence. It offers the thing many of us feel is most lacking in our lives today: purpose. Imagine owning a business selling things you really believe in, constantly developing new skills that allow you to improve what you do. Imagine a career that didn't require years of expensive training but that focused on the "soft skills" of building relationships with people in your community. That's what network marketing offers.

It's also an incredible business opportunity for companies developing new products. Traditionally, companies have to work with distributors who take a huge cut of their revenue and limit where customers can find those products. Network marketing blows that whole system up by allowing people to sell those products themselves to everyone they feel might be interested.

So network marketing offers a better lifestyle, more money, purpose, and new opportunities for product developers. That's a powerful case for this business model to take over the world, and I haven't even brought up all the advantages.

A ROAD MAP TO THE MOON

For all those incredible reasons to jump into network marketing, I understand the hesitancy to enter this profession. This wasn't my first job either. I started out as an IT entrepreneur. In fact, long before I ever considered this profession, I had already scaled a very successful business. But I wasn't very satisfied with the work. I was making very good money, but I'd entered IT because it was the obvious path to wealth.

In fact, I'd taken this path because it was what was expected of me. I'm the son of second-generation Italian immigrants in Switzerland. Like lots of kids in that situation, I grew up with parents who were hardworking, disciplined, and focused on lifting our family up. My grandparents had arrived in Switzerland with nothing. My parents had done everything they could to raise our family up. The end result was an expectation I'd go into a traditional career path with the potential to firmly plant our family in the middle class or above. And I dutifully did just that. But after years of success, looking around one day, I realized my heart just wasn't in it.

So I went looking for an opportunity I could really believe in. When I heard about network marketing at first, I was curious. The results I saw were quite good, but I felt there was some real untapped potential that could take a network marketing business to whole new heights. I wanted something I could really put everything into. Most of what I learned about the profession early on was the same info you've probably come across. It could get me some extra cash on the side, or it might be a good one-time payday, but that was it. At most, it might represent a decent income stream, with the real riches saved for the people who happened to enter the business early.

I wanted something more ambitious.

But I didn't abandon the idea entirely. Instead, I kept reading and investigating. Since I have a natural inclination for numbers, I began entering figures that would represent the hypothetical growth suggested in *The 45-Second Presentation That Will Change Your Life* by Don Failla.

As I looked over the results, that's when it hit me. Everyone made these claims about network marketing because they were looking at it all wrong. Network marketing wasn't a side hustle; it was ***an innovative new opportunity to build a real business***.

As soon as I saw the potential of network marketing, I literally said out loud, ***"Mamma mia, if I'm right about this, this is the best unknown secret in the whole business world!"***

If I was right, the potential was almost unlimited.

That's why we're going to the moon with this book. I'm not trying to help you get a business venture to just take off. I don't want you struggling to keep some organization hovering just off the ground. I want you soaring beyond the atmosphere. The moon is where the millionaires and billionaires of the world want to go. So that's our aim too.

I know that the moon feels far away—probably about as far away as a million dollars sounds to most people reading this. Network marketing tends to attract people who feel lost in their career. They don't like their jobs, or they aren't making enough. Or maybe they took some time off to focus on family, and they don't know how to get back into a full-time career again. To anyone in that situation, just making "good" money or even "okay" money sounds like more than they could ever hope for at the moment.

That's totally understandable, and if you're just looking for "good" money, I'm sure there's a lot you can get from this book. But it isn't my main focus here. Instead, I want to speak directly to those who feel good isn't good enough.

If you think you have it in you to shoot for the moon, then here's how we're going to do it in this book.

We'll start the way all astronauts start, by learning the basics and training for the trip. In the first part of this book, I've laid out a basic understanding of network marketing, its potential, and how to make sure you're set up for success. From there, we have to build the rocket. That can take years depending on how you do it, but I've developed a one-month process to get your whole network marketing operation up and running.

With our rocket on the launch pad, we'll add the rocket fuel. This is the most powerful business tool in the network marketing profession: the ninety-day run. I'll show you how to organize one to really get your business growing.

After that, we'll take off, leave the atmosphere, maintain our course for the moon, and once we land, set ourselves up to conquer the whole solar system with the team we've built.

The ideas ahead are easy enough to understand, even if you're completely new to business. But again, they are going to take some work to implement. Astronauts train hard. No one thinks getting to the moon is easy. If you follow all the advice in this book, though, I'm confident you can get there yourself.

ARE YOU READY FOR LIFTOFF?

After only four months as a network marketer, I achieved the coveted diamond rank at my company. This is not the highest rank available, but it's the one everyone shoots for. You can think of it as the best sign you've "arrived." On the fourth anniversary of that event this year, I sent a message to all my entrepreneurial friends who had so far scoffed at my decision:

> To all of you who aren't considering it yet, my company is now 26X in sales from that time. We do in a day what we used to do in a month. My personal commission has increased 30X. Show me any other business opportunity that offers that kind of return with such a small initial investment.

This kind of unbelievable growth was only possible because I built my business through network marketing. That's why Robert Kiyosaki, the author of *Rich Dad, Poor Dad*, was right when he called network marketing **the business model of the twenty-first century**. If you see network marketing as a profession, as a business you put the time in to build and maintain for many years to come, you can achieve anything you would with any other business model—and you can do it faster and at less cost.

If you do the right things, it doesn't matter when you start in this business or who you know; you can achieve the outrageous success you've always dreamed of. Success in this profession is determined not by when you get in but by the work you do and how you do it. That's what makes it such an incredible opportunity!

I truly believe in this profession. I believe in its value, and I believe in its potential for those who are hungry and willing to do the work. We're aiming for the moon today, but we'll be heading for Neptune before you know it. And then, there's nothing stopping us from conquering the stars.

That's why I'm sharing with you everything you need to build your own rocket. It'd be irresponsible not to. I believe in really pushing this profession forward, and I believe you could be someone who could help us do that.

This is a mission for me. If you're ready to jump on board, then I want to be your NASA. For me, money isn't the goal; the journey is the goal.

So let's get ready for liftoff.

PART I

PREPARING THE LAUNCH PAD

CHAPTER 1

A TRUE MERITOCRACY

I didn't just hit rock bottom. I stood face-to-face with the collapse of a life I had built with discipline, logic, and everything I thought was "right." Everything around me—and inside me—felt heavy, unstable, and on the verge of breaking. I was emotionally drained, physically exhausted, and financially maxed out. I was in debt. Some months, I had no idea how I would pay the rent.

Then came the moment that shattered the illusion: a $500 fine for parking in the wrong place. To others, it might have seemed trivial. To me, it was the tipping point. I knew I couldn't go on like this.

I was a construction engineer—skilled, reliable, and successful on paper. My job gave me stability, structure, and recognition. But I needed more freedom, more purpose, more alignment, and, in that moment especially, more money.

I didn't want to keep surviving. And so, an old dream returned: network marketing. Years earlier, I had dipped my toes into this profession. I was hungry, driven, and willing to work, but I lacked the depth, the structure, and the leadership required for true success. I got lost in the noise. So I quit, disappointed and disillusioned.

When the opportunity came back around, I was skeptical. But something in me had changed. I had nothing left to lose and everything to gain.

That's when I met Sandro. For the first time, I had a system to match my vision, fire, and commitment. With my heart and my head aligned, I looked him in the eyes and said, "I will be your number one."

And I kept that promise. Today, I am the number one woman in the company.

My breakthrough came during the pandemic—a time when the world stood still. I saw what most missed: network marketing was no longer a side hustle. It was a solution. A movement. A path to independence, leadership, and generational wealth.

*In the time since that moment, I have built an international organization of over 50,000 people—rooted in clarity, excellence, and one guiding principle that still drives every decision I make: **People over Profit.***

—Marijana

NETWORK MARKETING AERODYNAMICS

Before blasting off for the moon, every astronaut has to fully understand their mission. They spend years studying physics and astronomy while also training for space travel. Then, they spend months pouring over every aspect of the specific mission ahead.

If we want to reach the moon with network marketing, we have to do something similar. We have to understand what network marketing is, its potential, its risks, and what is required of us for success. That's what we'll be doing in this first part of the book.

So let's start with that first point. Network marketing is a business model that completely upends how companies traditionally sell products. Most of the products you buy every day are created and manufactured by one large corporation that sells those products to another large corporation that then sells them to you. Some things you buy—often services but also some products you might get from Amazon, for instance—are sold directly from the company creating them to you.

Network marketing does things differently. Instead of selling through a store or directly through their website, *the company works with individuals and their own "network" of connections*. Those individuals *start their own business* selling the products to friends, family, coworkers, neighbors, and even strangers. They also "sponsor," or recruit, some of those individuals to join their business. As sponsors, they teach those new to the business everything they've learned so far. These new recruits then sell to all of their connections. And if they choose, they can also create their own business where they can sponsor more people to join.

This business model, like any business model, can be used for everything from creating genuine opportunities for all those involved to outright scams, as we'll discuss in a moment. But it's important to recognize here at the outset that this really is, at root, just a business model. The same way taking out loans and founding your own company with your own products that you sell directly to your customers is a business model or building a large corporation full of complex hierarchies that sell products to other businesses is a business model. These aren't good or bad on their own; it's all in how you use them.

What's unique about the network marketing model is that *it has so much unrealized potential*. Once you fully understand how it works, you'll see that it really could be the business model of the twenty-first century.

THE MYTH

To really dig into what network marketing is and how you can succeed in this profession, it's worth taking a moment to break down all the myths and misunderstandings that surround it.

Some myths have a way of circulating long after they're disproven. Some people still believe the earth is flat, despite all the evidence to prove we live on a sphere. Network marketing is surrounded by such myths.

The first and most common myth about network marketing is that it is a pyramid scheme. It's easy to see where this accusation comes from. In the first place, pyramid schemes and network marketing share certain features. And at the same time, there have been network marketing businesses that operated as pyramid schemes.

Before you throw down the book and give up on our mission, though, let me state emphatically: pyramid schemes and network marketing businesses are very distinct operations. A pyramid scheme involves a company that provides financial compensation by getting new people to pay a large amount to join the organization. The first people to join make their money once they convince others to join. Those people make money only once another round of people join. In these schemes, the only real source of revenue comes from the newest members of the organization—those at the bottom of the pyramid—who usually have to pay a lot of money to become part of the organization. That money is then funneled up, with each layer of the pyramid taking their cut until it reaches the top.

A Ponzi scheme works in a similar way, only with more of a focus on investment then high fees to join the organization. In each case, as soon as the business runs out of new subscribers/investors, the whole thing falls apart.

You can see how this could be confused with network marketing. Network marketing does involve bringing new recruits into the organization. There is always some amount of expense involved in becoming a member of these companies. And some amount of the revenue these new recruits generate goes to those who recruited them and further up the hierarchy.

However, crucially, legitimate network marketing companies use recruiting as only a single component of their business strategy. If recruiting stopped completely, the business wouldn't crumble—*because it's a legitimate business with real, legitimate products!* Instead, a real network marketing company would lose some revenue if it ended its subscription model, but it would still be a viable business.

Let's put some numbers behind this. I've heard of companies

in this profession that are indeed pyramid shaped. If you cut them off from new subscriptions, they'd lose 70 to 80 percent of their revenue in a month. But that's not the case with legitimate network marketing companies. If we stopped subscriptions, it would hurt. But we'd only lose about 8 percent of our revenue. That's a big chunk, undeniably, and we don't want to lose that revenue, of course. But we would still have a sustainable business in that case. The reason is people genuinely love the products we sell. We could sell them in stores or through the connections of the network marketers we already have and do just fine.

That's myth number one. Myth number two is that network marketing is a get rich quick strategy, particularly if what you really mean by that is get-rich-quick-and-get-out-quick. This is related to the myth that network marketing is a pyramid scheme. It only makes sense to view the profession in terms of getting in and getting out with easy money if the assumption is someone else will be left holding the bag.

But this isn't right either. Instead, as I recently saw the network marketing social media coach (and dear friend) Frazer Brookes suggest at an event in Turkey, it's better to think of network marketing as buying your way into a company on the ground floor and then making sure that investment pays off. **Network marketing is like buying stock in a company at $300 and then working hard to turn its value into $1 million over the next three or four years.**

If you could have invested a few hundred dollars in Apple in the early 2000s and taken a position in the company three years before the debut of the iPhone, would you have taken it? Of course! It would have taken a little money, a lot of time, and a lot of hard work, but the reward would have been immense.

That's the kind of deal on offer in network marketing.

THE TRUTH

I'll be completely honest with you. Network marketing has the potential to be all the things it's been accused of. Some companies and individuals have treated it as a get-rich-quick pyramid scheme in the past. Others have done the same thing using other business models, of course. Just look up Bernie Madoff, who ripped off people for billions. Some have suggested many tech companies have gotten rich using a sort of pyramid scheme to lure in investors.

Luckily, these network marketing scams tend to have tell-tale signs. We'll discuss how to recognize and avoid them in the next chapter.

For now, I want to point out that those schemes are the outliers. In reality, almost every time, **network marketing is the cheapest and easiest way to build your own business**. Usually, building a business requires loans, a new idea for a product or service, and an advanced understanding of best business practices. To make that business a success, you have to know how to build your product, price your product, market your product, and sell your product. That's a lot of information you have to learn, and you have to know it all before you actually start selling anything!

That's a wonderful model if you have a great idea for a new restaurant you're confident will be the most popular in town or an app that could end up on everyone's phone and you're comfortable taking a big risk. But that isn't for everyone.

What network marketing offers you is *the chance to work on your own terms, running your own business, without all those extra steps or extra risk*. The products or services are already developed. These companies already spent all the money to develop high quality services or products that they could sell either directly to customers or through a distributor like Walmart or Target. They choose to use the network marketing business model because it works best for their bottom line. Through one of these companies, *you can learn everything you need to know about running a business while you're running it*. And you can get assistance from your "upline"—the people who entered the business before you who are further "up" the business hierarchy.

As an aside, I use the word hierarchy in its traditional sense, which is just where people are placed in proximity to the core company and their products. It doesn't reflect overall success, which, as we'll discuss in a moment, is thoroughly meritocratic.

But other than those unique qualities, the way to succeed in network marketing is by recognizing the fact this is really where the difference with traditional entrepreneurship stops. Stated another way, *network marketing is really just another form of entrepreneurship*. That means you have to work as hard as an entrepreneur, dedicate yourself to the business as much as an entrepreneur, and be as ambitious and innovative as an entrepreneur.

When you do that, network marketing offers *the best possible upside for a new business owner. It's simply the best entrepreneurial idea out there.*

I know what I'm speaking about. I've built my own successful IT company from the ground up. I know what it takes to go the traditional entrepreneurship route. In fact, that company did very well financially. When I encountered network marketing, though, I realized the potential was off the charts. And I realized it on my own. No one was there trying to sell me on a rosy, idealized version of the business model. But no one was there to pour cold water on my ambitions either.

Instead, I ran the numbers myself, starting with those laid out in the *45-Second Presentation* by Don Failla. The fact I didn't have any knowledge about network marketing and didn't have a relationship with the company I would eventually partner with meant I was able to come up with my own interpretation of those numbers. No one was there to tell me what was realistic and to sell me on an unrealistic dream. I just put the numbers from the book in an Excel spreadsheet and ran some basic calculations. I soon realized that if I worked hard enough and achieved those numbers, I would hit diamond rank in four months. Within a year? The number was, frankly, ridiculous. I could hardly believe it.

Perhaps if I had had a sponsor at that time, they would have talked me out of such starry-eyed expectations. But there was no one looking over my shoulder, telling me what was possible. It was like someone a hundred years ago, looking up at the moon and thinking they could actually get there because no one was nearby to say such a feat was impossible.

And because I didn't know it was impossible, I did it. I hit my mark at four months and became a diamond manager, exactly as the numbers suggested I would in that Excel document. I didn't quite hit that second goal in one year. Humans, after all, are not as predictable as numbers in a document. But I hit it a few months after my first anniversary in my new business.

Since then, I've helped many others follow the same path to success. That's the true potential of network marketing.

A FAIR SHOT AT REAL SUCCESS

Neil Armstrong got to be the first person to walk on the moon not because he knew the right people or had the money to push himself to the front of the line. He was given that honor because he was the best astronaut and leader NASA had. NASA runs on a meritocracy. The organization recruits from the best US Air Force pilots and the best American scientists. From that team of elites, it then chooses the very best to send into space.

If you want to go to the moon, you have to prove you're the best. You have to work the hardest, show the most ingenuity, and bring the most passion. Nothing else will cut it.

Network marketing is a lot like that. Once you understand how the model really works, you can see that *it's a true meritocracy*. It doesn't matter where you come from, what color your skin is, or what your gender or sexuality is. If you show a talent for the work and you put the effort in, this business model will reward you. You will rise to the top almost every time.

Because it requires a limited financial investment, this path is available to people of any background. You can enter from almost anywhere on the planet and at any time—when you're twenty or sixty-five!

And despite what you might assume, it doesn't matter who you know. If you work hard, learn as you go, and follow the steps I've laid out in this book, your work can pay off—big!

COUNTDOWN CHECKLIST

3. Understand the definition of network marketing.

2. Recognize that network marketing is not a scam; it's a business model. And like all business models, there are scams and real opportunities out there.

1. The key to success in network marketing is seeing it as a meritocracy. The best rise to the top. It's up to you if you want to be one of the best.

GRADING YOUR PARTNER

I was already a network marketing veteran with eight years of experience when I came across what looked like an amazing opportunity. It was 2022, and my team was temporarily without a company. I was actively looking for a new opportunity. That's when I received a call from an acquaintance inviting me to Dubai. There, I was introduced to many of the people at the top of this organization. I personally knew some of the founders and members of the corporate team.

When they presented the business concept, everything sounded very plausible. Here's how the money flows in, here's how it's invested, and here's how we all make a profit. They pointed out all the people in their organization already making a lot of money.

With all my experience, I felt confident that I knew a good opportunity when I saw one. I knew what worked, what didn't, and what to look for when choosing a network marketing partner. This business seemed to check all the right boxes.

Despite checking those boxes, though, even in that first meeting, I had an uneasy feeling about the whole thing. Something seemed...off. But I pushed those feelings to one side and decided to join up.

For the first thirteen or fourteen months, everything ran smoothly. But over time, the money stopped flowing, and investors couldn't access their funds. Gradually, the truth emerged: the whole company was a well-disguised Ponzi scheme. The early joiners earned money, while the latecomers lost— heavily. And my team and I had joined too late. The founder ended up disappearing with billions, and to this day, no one knows where he is.

Even with my years of experience, I'd allowed myself to be swayed by friendly relationships and a first glance at the business model. I learned a valuable lesson that day. In network marketing—a beautiful but often misused profession—double-checking everything is essential.

Luckily, my business and I have recovered since. And these days, I focus only on companies with real products, real value, transparent leadership, and a business model where average people have a real chance to achieve long-term, above-average success.

—KEVIN G.

WATCH OUT FOR SCAMS

Not every rocket makes it to outer space, even when designed and built by the best experts in the world. Things can go wrong, and there are no guarantees in life. But those experts have the best possible record for building rockets that launch successfully and get where they're going. So if you want to get to the moon yourself, you really want to work with a company that is in the business of helping people build the best rockets—and a company with a great record of successful launches. That means you have to be ready to evaluate the quality of the company you partner with.

In doing this evaluation, you should be aware of two major risks in choosing your network marketing company. The first is the one everyone thinks about. To be completely blunt, while network marketing is not a scam, there are real scams out there. These are companies that make big promises but are built to pay as little as possible out. At some point, these companies collapse overnight and take all the profits with them.

It's absolutely essential, then, that you protect yourself from these scams.

Thankfully, there are a number of signs you can look out for that can tell you a company might be a network marketing scam. The first of those signs is huge promises with nothing behind them. There's a lot of potential for incredible wealth and success in network marketing—as I've already suggested in this book—but some companies use this potential to hide the poor quality of their products or to paper over a payment system that funnels all the money you make back to the top.

Often these claims feel too good to be true. Consider the difference between a company that says that you could make six figures a year if you work very hard for a few years versus "You'll double your investment in under twelve months" or "You'll be rich and make money while doing nothing." One suggests you can make it to the moon; the other promises you the sun and stars without even needing a rocket.

These scammers often spend a lot of time and most of their brochure space providing long descriptions of the future lifestyle you could enjoy if you work with them. What is in short supply is information about the products you'll be selling or the actual system that allows you to make all this money.

Along with big promises and little clarity, these companies often ask for large financial investments upfront. While there's always some costs that come with joining an organization, these companies often demand new subscribers invest thousands of dollars in their products in order to join.

Importantly, some companies can justify this level of upfront investment. I know of one network marketing company that sells water filters. A general rule of network marketing is you should own a product before you sell it since this helps you introduce that product to your connections. However, unless we're talking about a "high-ticket product," the goal is to avoid stacking products in your basement when you get started. If a company expects you to buy thousands of dollars of supplements or makeup at the outset, you should consider looking elsewhere.

This leads to a more complicated form of due diligence you will want to do with your prospective company: investigating the product and the company's origin. Another general rule of network marketing is that the model works better with products than services. If your company is offering a service, you need to be extra sure it's one your connections can't get elsewhere for cheaper or free. I've seen network marketing companies that sell educational services that were no better than information you could find on YouTube for free. This was a classic example of a company existing solely to build up that pyramid scheme. The only real source of revenue for the company was getting people to sign up and pay for the educational product themselves.

If your company is selling a product, investigate if it is high quality enough to justify the price and create real demand from your connections. Does it have a tangible, unique selling point? Is there something it offers that customers won't get elsewhere?

Ultimately, you want to determine whether this company could stand solely on its sales because of the quality of what it offers. If it no longer brought in subscriptions from new recruits into the organization, do you believe it would still be a successful business? If not, you are their true source of revenue. Watch out!

One final warning sign of a scam is the origin of the company. Beware new businesses with websites registered in weird locations. Find out who the owners are. What is their story? Where are they based? How long have they been in business? How did they come up with their products?

These are basic considerations anyone investing in a company would ask, and since, as we already know, you are investing in this company while also working with them, you have to ask them too. Consider yourself a savvy investor looking for the next big thing. Ask all the questions you think that investors would to make them comfortable putting their money into a business.

IS THIS A PYRAMID SCHEME?

I know the above section is a lot to take in, but since this is a really important topic, I want to spend a little more time making sure you don't end up investing your time and money in a scam instead of a legitimate network marketing company.

With that in mind, I want to break down the signs a company is a scam into a few basic bullet points with questions you should ask before signing up:

- **How much do I have to pay upfront?** If a network marketing company sells products for $50 each, you shouldn't be required to spend thousands of dollars to sign up. That's a sign you're the real source of revenue, not the people you and your team sell products to.
- **Is this really high quality?** Many scams in this space repackage cheap products and try to sell them for top dollar. They take faux leather jackets you can get on Alibaba for $10 each and try to sell them as high-end, handmade, real leather jackets.
- **Does the product sell itself?** There's a difference in how a cheap used car salesperson and a luxury car salesperson behaves. The used car salesperson will do anything to get you to buy one of their cars right now. They use every trick in the book. The luxury car salesperson is laid back. If you want the car, you'll take it. If not, someone else is going to buy it. So how are people in this network marketing company selling their products? Do they seem to believe it's a quality item or are they pushing aggressively to try to force every sale?
- **Is there a market for this stuff?** Scams often sell items that are either really niche (with a small market of potential customers) or that can be found everywhere (which means the market is oversaturated). You should be able to tell right away by gut instinct if a company is selling something that

lots of people want and that lots of people can't get elsewhere for a better price. All of these questions address the most common scam in the network marketing field, what I call the "product as an alibi." These scammers put together some kind of product offering just as an excuse to claim they're a legitimate business. They make most of their money from recruiting people like you and getting you to buy up tons of their inventory. And that leads to perhaps the most important question you have to ask yourself:

- **Does it matter when I join up?** This is perhaps the biggest difference between a pyramid scheme and a real, legitimate network marketing company. In a pyramid scheme, you have to get in early because as soon as the scammers run out of new recruits, the whole thing collapses. The only people who get rich are those who get in first. It's a race to jump in quickly and get out before it's too late. In network marketing, it doesn't matter when you join. If you sign up with a company that's ten years old, you have just as much of a chance of reaching the moon and becoming a millionaire as the person who signed up on day one. You should only join a company where you feel you can answer all these questions satisfactorily.

SOME COMPANIES NEVER LET YOU LEAVE

Scams aren't the only way a network marketing company can limit your horizons. Some companies are fully legitimate with real products and a business model that is meant to benefit those who work with them. However, their model, for one reason or another, never actually lets you get rich or achieve sustainable success. You work hard, but the company reaps most of the reward instead of sharing it through the network.

This is far harder to catch than the scams I've described above—partly because it isn't always intentional. This actually happened with the company I work with. They had a glass ceiling on potential earnings that they didn't realize existed. In December 2021, I hit a rank no one else had ever hit. When I reviewed my income in March 2022, I discovered that over the past three months, I had been making $3,000 less than before I reached that level.

I spoke up to those running the company, and they looked at their formula. It turned out, the distribution of sales income was shaped like an onion. The company wanted a lot of people in the middle ranks—where they were making $6,000 to $12,000 a month. They simply hadn't thought to build out their incentives beyond that income range. After our discussion, they changed their system.

To make sure your company is offering the chance to get to the moon, ask your sponsor or a company representative about the top five or ten earners in the business. How long have they been there? How much are they making? Find out about the historical growth numbers for those who enter the company, do well, and keep growing.

Now, I want to be clear that there will definitely be some variation here depending on how your company is organized and the size of the business. The top earner at one of our company's chief competitors makes three times less than me. And he's been doing this for almost thirty years longer. But he's also still doing extremely well for himself! So long as those top earners are making the kind of money you envision for yourself and there's a history of people making it to that level, then that's a good partner for you.

The real risk here is getting involved with a company that limits your potential—to the point you can never make enough to really do this full-time or that most of your income dries up if you ever stop hustling. Any good network marketing company should be providing between 15 and 3 percent commission on your sales. That number will go down as you sell more, but you still earn more because it's a piece of a larger pie.

So long as there's room to grow to the position you want to get to—to land you on the moon—then that's a company you should consider joining.

Along with proving there's potential to reach the moon with their organization, you want your company to have the structure to support you as well. There should be a clear organizational structure that your sponsor can show you that lays out the entire upline from you up to the person running the operation. That way, you can always reach someone to help you when you have a question or a problem.

SIGNS YOU'RE WORKING WITH NASA

An astronaut is only as good at the organization they work for. I'm sure there have been plenty of great potential astronauts born around the world, but if their countries lacked a good space program—and they didn't go work with another country's program—they never left the ground. The same is true in network marketing. It doesn't matter how much potential you have or how hard you're willing to work if you put all that talent and effort into a scam or a company designed to limit your income.

But if the company is free of all the concerns I've laid out above, the only qualifier remaining is whether it speaks to you. If you're working with a product-based company with a quality offering for their customers, all that matters is if that product excites you. ***It's really important in network marketing that you care about the product at least as much as the potential upgrade in your lifestyle.***

Network marketing has a lot to do with trust. People need to trust that you care about what you're selling and that you want them to join you in selling.

Your network marketing business should roughly divide its time and focus like this: 50 percent sales and 50 percent recruitment. If that's the break down, your feelings about the product really matter!

So if you don't care about perfume or supplements, don't work with a company with those core products. The world of network marketing is enormous these days. Find something you're passionate about and get behind the best company in that area.

COUNTDOWN CHECKLIST

3. Know the signs a network marketing company might be a scam.

2. Look into your company's payment scheme to make sure you can achieve your financial goals there.

1. If everything else looks good, choose your network marketing partner based on the products you find most interesting.

MOONSHOT MENTALITY

As a third-generation immigrant, I was brought up to believe in discipline and hard work. My grandparents had moved to Switzerland in the '60s, back when Italy was still recovering from the War. They'd arrived with almost nothing, and it had been their mission—and then my parents' mission after them—to haul the family up to the comfortable middle class.

So hard work wasn't just idle talk in my family. I was expected to put all my effort into excelling. No excuses. And this expectation was placed on me from a very early age. When I was in grade school, one of my teachers assigned our class an essay every Monday. The topic was always the same. All we had to do was write a page or so about our weekend. The first few weeks, I came in without any preparation and tried to put my essay together in class. I didn't do well. My teacher had a habit of collecting essays in the order he assumed would be worst to best. My essays were collected near the beginning, meaning my teacher knew I was a poor writer.

Once my mother found out about these essays, I was no longer allowed to just show up and wing them. Instead, I was forbidden to go out and play on Sundays until I had not only written a draft of the essay but memorized it. I would have to sit there for hours working on those sentences. Making things all the more difficult, I'm left-handed, and my mother demanded perfect penmanship. So the writing itself was time consuming, even before I began memorizing what I'd written.

But that hard work paid off. Once I started preparing, I shot to the top of the class. My teacher stopped collecting my essays first. After a few weeks, mine was the very last he would gather up.

At the time, as a kid, I resented having to do that extra work, but my mom was right to push me. Out of those Sunday afternoon essay writing sessions, I developed a work ethic that has led me to amazing levels of success. I used that work ethic to grow my IT company. And I brought it to network marketing to become one of the most successful network marketing entrepreneurs in history.

—SANDRO

SKILLS ISSUE

I tell this story because I want to make it clear that I was not born with all the skills necessary to succeed in business. However, I had learned to work hard as a child, and I had all the qualities I needed to succeed in network marketing.

This is one of the most unique aspects of network marketing. Where business usually requires you to develop a set of skills before you even enter the profession, network marketing allows you to learn as you go.

Think of all the qualities you have to possess if you want to become successful through one of the traditional business routes. Whether it's traditional entrepreneurship, sales, or becoming an executive, you need to master a number of qualities before you can really start rising up the career ladder. You'll have to be *a people person*—someone who can connect to others in your office, including bosses and direct reports. You'll have to be able to build relationships with vendors and suppliers, customers and investors. If you don't have those people skills when you start out, how are you going to get anywhere?

The same is true for being *good with numbers*. Whether you're running your own business, taking sales, or presenting to the board, you have to be able to work the math to make sure you know how your business is doing on multiple levels.

Relatedly, you'll need *a strong business sense*. You'll need to have a feel for marketing, hiring, management, and product development. Otherwise, you'll get left behind by the competition.

You'll need to be *reliable*: someone that colleagues and customers alike can trust to follow through on every promise. If you say you're going to be somewhere at 11:00 a.m., you have to be there, every time. If you say a shipment will arrive on Monday by 3:00 p.m., it better be there.

You have to master all this going in, and that's before we even consider the technical knowledge you need for certain careers. You may need years of expensive training and an apprenticeship of some sort. Those are the requirements for entry. It's a heavy burden, and that's why so many get left out.

LEARN BY DOING

You will eventually need to develop those same skills in network marketing, but this profession has a better strategy to help you develop them. Instead of having to study and invest upfront before you can make a single dollar, you can join network marketing today and *learn by doing*.

The only requirements to do this grow out of that work ethic that I developed as a kid. As the great network marketing coach Eric Worre puts it, the qualities you need to bring to network marketing are being *willing, hungry, and coachable*.

Let's break each of those down.

- **Willing:** Those who succeed in network marketing want it so badly, nothing can stop them. If someone is really willing, you can see it in how they approach each task. Whether they're sick or busy or tired, they find a way to get it done—and they get it done well and quickly. Every time you're feeling lazy, willingness pushes you forward through to that next step.
- **Hungry:** Network marketing isn't for the easily satisfied. Those who do well here are driven for real, radical success. This hunger is partly materialistic, but it's deeper than that. They aren't looking for a few extra bucks; they want something more out of life. They have passion, intensity, ambition, and they've just been looking for somewhere to put all that energy. They want to live their life to the fullest.
- **Coachable:** Those who do well in this profession are open to new ideas. Because they're willing and hungry, they'll always do what it takes, so they're eager to accept assignments, eager to get feedback, and eager to try things a better

way. This is so important because this is the quality that allows you to develop all the skills I mentioned above. It also saves you time. You don't need to reinvent the wheel here; others have already developed the system. You just have to learn from the best and ace every task.

With these qualities in place, you can **grow and learn and challenge yourself** even as you build your own business in real time.

Worre's three qualities will take you very far in this industry, but I'd like to add one more before we move on. All the great network marketers I know share a fourth quality: **consistency**.

You have to be willing to put the time in and do the hard work over and over again. This is what really separates those who only manage to take off with network marketing from those who actually reach the moon.

What does consistency look like? Here's a really dramatic example.

Last year at a Go Pro event, I was on stage with Eric and a number of network marketers. Eric asked us how many days off we took off in the previous year. Everyone around me was bragging about the months they took off. My answer was different. Sheepishly, I said I took ten days.

Afterward, I had to admit I had lied. The truth was that I took *zero days off*. Every day of the year, I worked on my business. Sure, I took vacations with my family and laid around on the beach for several weeks. But I still fit in meetings and planned strategy on those days. I was still available for calls when needed.

Now, perhaps my level of consistency is over the top. It might be a bit too obsessive. But the closer you are to those ten days off than the ninety, the better your results.

And it doesn't matter if you do this from the top of a penthouse apartment, a Caribbean beach, or on an Alpine slope. Work from wherever you want. Work whatever hours you want. But you have to work on this business consistently.

When you combine these four qualities, the skills above will develop naturally as you develop your business. You will learn to be more of a people person. You'll learn how to work with numbers. You'll cultivate that powerful business sense. *All it takes is getting started in network marketing while being willing, hungry, coachable, and consistent.*

FOLLOW THE FORMULA

Actually, there's one other related quality you need for success in network marketing—and any kind of entrepreneurship—*obsession*.

I have a friend, Samuel, whose ambition is to completely disrupt the industry of fine pens. His company sells them, and he also spends significant time and energy creating awareness about the value of his field. He's obsessed with his work. When other people are sitting around talking about what's on TV, he's sitting around thinking about how he can create further awareness around the world of fine pens.

We're all used to the idea of the obsessed business owner. We've seen people like Steve Jobs, who dedicated everything to designing the iPhone. What you don't often hear, though, is that you aren't born with this level of obsession. ***The work becomes an obsession over time.*** The more you work, the more success you see, and the bigger your goals get. This creates a virtuous cycle that keeps reinforcing that growing hunger. It's like going to the gym. The more you go, the more you want to go. As you lose weight, gain muscle, and feel better, you become obsessed with getting back to the treadmill or the weight bench.

Once you start seeing success, it becomes addicting. And it fuels your motivation to keep improving. You do the work until you reach your limit and then you find the way to reach the next level.

Importantly, this doesn't mean that all you do is work or think about work. You can still focus on your family and have time with friends. But when it comes to work, you're locked in and giving everything.

The problem for many people is that they just don't know the path that leads to cultivating these qualities. Whether it's getting in shape or starting a business, they don't know what steps they should follow that will allow them to learn the necessary skills or become obsessed with their work.

I certainly felt this way when I approached getting in shape. As a child, I was bad at sports—so bad my gym teacher actually explicitly told me I sucked. I used to try to avoid gym class every day. If I could convince a teacher or a nurse I was sick for that period, it was a major win.

As I got older, I realized I wanted to feel healthier and stronger, but I didn't really know how to do it. I'd jog or lift weights, but it didn't seem to make much difference. Eventually, at around twenty-five, I decided I wanted to really try and do things right. I got a personal trainer, and I committed to getting into shape.

In our first session, I mentioned my frustrations. I tried to eat well, I told him. I worked out. But I never saw results. As I finished my little rant, my trainer laughed and said, "Sandro, this is why you hired me. Switch off your brain and just do what I tell you."

So I did. I worked out twice a day. I ran on an empty stomach. I ate what I was told, when I was told. Some of it was fun. I hated a lot of it. But in the end, *it worked*. After a few months, I had a six pack. I never thought that was possible.

This is what I'm trying to offer you in this book. To reach that level of obsession and to develop the skills you need for success, *you just have to turn off your brain and follow every step I'm going to lay out for you in the coming chapters*.

If you do that, over the next six months, you will build a business, you'll be well on your way to developing those critical network marketing skills, and you'll become obsessed. By the time you look up and look around you, you'll realize you're already well on your way to the moon.

COUNTDOWN CHECKLIST

3. Network marketing requires four qualities for success. You have to be willing, hungry, coachable, and consistent. The rest you can learn along the way.

2. With a little success, it's easy to become obsessed with your business. That's a good thing!

1. The best way to cultivate those skills and find success in network marketing is to turn your brain off and follow every step in this book exactly as I describe them.

PART II

BUILDING YOUR ROCKET

········· CHAPTER 4 ·········

CREATING A
FOUNDATION

When I decided to dive into the world of network marketing, I was a blank slate. With nothing more than a burning desire for more in life, I took a leap into the unknown and hoped for the best.

Amazingly, that bold step immediately paid off. Within just four months, I had a team of over five hundred people—an incredible success that I attributed mainly to my instinctive understanding of the business and my hard work. I had acted on intuition, without a clear strategy, and it all seemed to be working out.

Six months later, my team had reached a proud one thousand members. But my initial euphoria had started to evaporate in the face of reality. Instead of excitement, I felt enormously overwhelmed, as I suddenly realized I was responsible for a large group of people, all with different needs and expectations. I struggled through the daily calls and Zoom meetings where I often felt unprepared and insecure. I could see this was affecting our entire team dynamic.

For a while, I continued on without making any changes. I was earning a considerable income, and I still believed that my business's rise would be unstoppable.

Then summer came—and with it, an unexpected crash. Sales dropped drastically, many of my team members left, and I began to feel haunted by fear and uncertainty. I chased after people, trying to hold on to them, but they kept slipping away. In this difficult period, there were many moments when I wanted to quit. Thankfully, the will that had always driven me remained strong.

To turn things around, I needed an outside perspective. Having Sandro at my side as a mentor was invaluable. Sandro's presence gave me a sense of security when I felt overwhelmed. It was through observing him that I realized my problems stemmed from my lack of business structure. I marveled at his structured approach and ability to set priorities. I saw how important it is to consciously take time for planning and organization.

To stabilize my work habits, I sent him my daily to-do lists for a while. This routine not only helped me work in a more focused manner but also gave me a sense of accountability.

This was important because implementing a more systematic, structured approach to my business felt in many ways like starting over. I had to develop a strategy for training and educating team members. As I did so, I realized that I not only had to train my team but also work on my own development.

I also came to see that I should have been paying more attention to the relationships within the business. Those daily unstructured calls weren't enough. I needed to build in time to really get to know my team. That was crucial to building trust and a sense of community. So I identified *some motivated individuals in the team and made a point of visiting them after the summer.*

With more structure and some allies within the team, I then overhauled the process behind my daily calls, developing strategic topics to give each call a clear focus.

Once all this was in place, I turned back to recruitment. Even though I was plagued by fears that it would all go wrong again, I knew I had to bring new members into the business to move forward again. Thankfully, I was able to move past those concerns because I knew I now had the discipline and routines to succeed for myself and the team.

That time was one of the most challenging periods of my life—but it was also one of the most instructive. When I look back today, I feel proud. I realize that I had to go through those phases to become the person I am today, ready for any challenge. I also learned some valuable lessons: in particular, the importance of structure and process when building a network marketing business.

—Manuela

SLOW DOWN TO SPEED UP

The biggest risk early in your network marketing career is the one you may least expect: **it's going too quickly at the start**. This is an understandable reaction. You're about to launch your own company! You love these products, and you know other people are going to feel the same way! You're dreaming of landing on the moon and earning more money than you ever have before!

For all those reasons, though, **it's easy to start speeding through some really important early steps that are critical for your** *success*. That's why I recommend you take this first week and think of it like the first week at any other job you've ever had. I know, that's a bummer, but slowing down now ensures you learn what you need to learn and avoid making mistakes you can't fix.

Jumping into network marketing without this first week can lead to burning through all of your best connections and even losing faith in the entire business model just because you didn't know what you were doing. It's far better, then, to sit down and go through this orientation.

That first day on a new job can feel excruciatingly slow. All you want to do is actually get to work, and instead you have to sign paperwork, watch videos, do the training, and get to know all the people on your team. No one is going to let you get to work until you do all that.

It's the same with network marketing. **You can't skip anything**, no matter how much you want to jump into selling products or recruiting people into your business. You have to slow down now so you can go fast later. Trust me, you'll be breaking the sound barrier sooner than you think—in fact, you'll be speeding along in a matter of days!

Crucially, this is about speed but not eagerness. Eagerness is great! In fact, it's often the quality that tells sponsors who really has what it takes in this business. But you can be eager and still go at the pace that best prepares you to develop the right skills and become a success.

Consider how long it takes a hairdresser before they get to cut an important customer's hair. If you decided to become a hair-dresser, you wouldn't be handed a pair of scissors to cut that customer's hair for *months*. First, you'd watch an experienced stylist cut hair. Then, you'd start cutting wigs on mannequins. After a few weeks of practice, you'd get to cut the hair of some of your friends. Even after you proved you could cut hair on a real human, you'd still have to take on a number of lower-end customers before you'd finally be allowed to take a shot doing the work you wanted to be doing all along.

Remember, my key insight into network marketing—the one that allowed me to succeed in this field—was to treat it as a business and a profession. Professionals train and learn so they can outperform everyone else. The time you spend training is a big part of what will differentiate you from the amateur network marketers out there.

Network marketing moves much faster than that. But you still have to learn the ropes. In our case, this first week in particular, you have to exercise a little patience.

WHAT COUNTS AS A DAY?

Before we jump into the actual day-by-day, step-by-step process of building your rocket/business, I want to take a quick moment and explain how I've broken these steps down.

For the entirety of this part of the book, we'll be breaking tasks down into the days over which you'll complete them. *Importantly, most of these tasks don't require a full eight- or nine-hour day's work. Instead, you'll want to accomplish all the tasks in each section over that number of days.*

I know it's possible to go faster here. You could do all of week one's work in a single day if you dedicated the time to it. However, again, I don't want you to rush here. Instead, *if you finish your tasks ahead of time, go deeper instead of faster*. If you've finished everything for days one and two, for instance, focus on learning more about your company and its products. Watch more of their videos on YouTube. Do some research on the company's history. Reach out to your sponsor and ask some additional questions. You can also take a couple hours and just really digest all this new information. Take notes on what you've learned, write down any questions you have, and make sure you fully assimilate the information.

You want to stick to this rhythm, trust me. **It's been tried and tested thousands of times.** This is the same cadence I set up for new subscribers to my team. If you want to get to the moon, you don't build a rocket in a day. You make sure every part is in its right place. And this is how you do it.

DAY 1–2: SETTING UP YOUR BUSINESS

When I subscribe someone, I give them forty-eight hours to get acquainted with the basics of the business. This is your standard onboarding period when you figure out who to go to with questions and what you're going to be doing with your business.

Across these two days, you'll want to achieve all of these objectives:

- Meet your sponsor and upline.*
- Install any company apps.
- Learn about the business model and code of conduct.
- Go through any company startup checklists.
- Write down the skills you believe you possess that will help you in network marketing.
- Write down what your moon landing looks like: What is your ultimate goal as a network marketer? How much money do you need to make in order to achieve that goal?
- Place your first order.

Some of these steps will take no more than a minute. You can find and download an app while waiting in line to buy your groceries. And you can probably place your order in a matter of a few clicks. Others will take a bit more time. But each is important in its own right.

Each step here is designed to settle you into your company, to find your footing as a network marketing entrepreneur, and to set your sights on your ultimate goal. With that in mind, it may be best to tackle these steps in an organized and professional manner: sitting at a desk for an extended period when you can focus on the tasks at hand.

Getting to know your sponsor and upline will allow you to become familiar with the people you'll rely on when you have questions. These are the people who are going to show you

---

* You can visit www.sandrocazzato.com/moonshot to download a step-by-step guide so you don't skip any parts of the process. There are also additional materials to give more nuance to the ideas in this book. But be sure to read the whole book first so you understand the essence of the system before getting into some of those important details!

the ropes. But if you spend some time going over the company checklist and reviewing the business model and code of conduct, you'll have fewer—and probably better—questions anyway.

Don't rush through that information, though. The business model will explain how you're going to get paid, and the code of conduct will tell you how the company expects you to behave and how others should behave toward you.

Beyond those concerns, this is also your first opportunity to personalize your company. For instance, it's your chance to dig into the qualities you bring to the table right now. As we've already discussed, network marketing allows you to learn by doing, so you don't have to know everything upfront. But *you probably have skills that give you an edge from day one*. When I started, I looked to my experience in IT entrepreneurship. I had a good sense of how to run a business already. I knew how to organize a meeting and how to hire people. I could recognize talent when I saw it. And though I wasn't an extroverted people person, I was used to getting up in front of small groups and talking.

That list not only showed me the skills I could rely on immediately, it also showed me where I needed to grow. I did need to get better with one-on-one interactions, for instance.

A second list you'll want to start immediately is your actual ambitions for this business. Where do you want this ship to take you? Everyone is aiming for the moon, but we aren't all trying to land in the same spot. Maybe you want to be making a million dollars a year. Or maybe you don't care about making that much, and you just want to be the master of your time while making more than you do in your current job. Whatever your dream moon destination, start thinking about it now and start writing it down.

Crucially, when you write down your dreams and ambitions here, you should tie them to a dollar amount. Start with what you want your life to look like, and then work backward to the amount you would have to earn to live that life.

If your ultimate goal is simply to earn enough to quit your current job and work in a business you run yourself, then you need to be making at least the same amount you make right now. If you have bigger goals—say, you want to move into a three-bedroom apartment in New York City or Paris and travel first-class three times a year—find out how much that costs. That number is your ultimate goal.

Once again, don't rush here. Don't just write the first thought that comes to mind about your skills or your dreams just so you can check a task off. Give this some deep thought. You have two days! Take the time to get this right—it can make a huge difference!

I recently met a woman in Kosovo who had been treading water in her network marketing business for years. I asked her what she really wanted to achieve in this profession.

"I want to make enough that my parents can retire and enjoy the rest of their lives."

"Wonderful," I said. "How much would that cost?"

After she gave me a confused look, I helped her break it down.

She told me her parents spend about $3,000 a month. That's $36,000 a year net, or around $72,000 a year before taxes. For her parents to retire and be free of financial worry, she'd need to make enough for them to live on that amount for perhaps another twenty years.

"That means you need about $1.4 million."

I could immediately see a spark in her eyes. For the first time in who knows how long, she had a real reason to invest more time and energy into her business. She had a real target to aim for—and that can add a whole lot of motivation to keep going and keep growing.

DAY 3-4: CREATING YOUR NETWORK

If the first two days were onboarding, in these next two you're training for your new role taking over your business. This is the time when you start the process that will result in actual sales, subscriptions, and income.

- Build your contact list of 150 people.
- Break them down into warm and cold relationships.
- Learn the invitation script and practice it.
- Learning how to contact and invite effectively.

I know a lot of you probably think at the moment that you don't have 150 contacts, but that's almost always false. I've seen people get on stage with the network marketing guru, Eric Worre, insisting they don't know even fifty people. But all it took to change their mind was a quick scroll through their phones. In moments, they realized they had hundreds of connections. The key here is expanding your sense of who counts as a contact. These aren't just family and friends but neighbors, coworkers, and even people you have had a couple conversations with on social media.

At this point, *everyone your life touches should go on the list*. To make sure everyone is there, browse your Instagram, Facebook, and WhatsApp accounts. Look through your emails. Take a walk in your neighborhood and write down the names of all your neighbors. You don't have to be a stalker about it, but if you regularly say hi and wave at certain neighbors, put them down on the list.

If you are still falling short of that 150, don't worry too much. If you view network marketing as a growing entrepreneurial business, *you don't have to constantly lean on your existing relationships*. You'll be making brand new contacts before you know it.

However, the difference between people who succeed in network marketing and those who don't is how thoughtful and purposeful this list is. So take it seriously.

Once you have the list, organize it from your warmest relationships to your coldest. At the top of the list, then, are the people you know best. That probably includes family and your best friends. From there, you have your other friends, more distant relatives, and then acquaintances and coworkers. Further down the list go the people you regularly have a quick friendly conversation with at the gym or the guy who works at your favorite restaurant who knows your order by heart. Finally, at the bottom, you can put those people you chatted with a couple times on Instagram or know through a friend of a friend.

Once again, **don't be afraid to add these really distant connections**. Put everyone on the list. **Don't decide for them if they'd want to be a customer or distributor!**

Now that you have your list, I want you to do something extremely important: put it down. I can't emphasize this enough—**do not contact anyone yet!**

Here's the reason why. Think of each of these contacts as your potential startup capital for your business. Each of them represents real potential dollars that could help you get this rocket off the ground. This is money you need to build some momentum and grow a larger operation.

The social media coach Frazer Brookes suggests putting an actual dollar value on these contacts. He even has a formula: take all the commissions you've made so far, divide it by how many you've sponsored in the business, and you know how much you could make from that contact long-term.

In my case, one contact has the potential to bring me $25,000 over the course of our business relationship. If you haven't sold a product or sponsored anyone yet, let's set your number lower and say each contact has the potential value of $1,000. Put that way, **are you willing to risk a thousand bucks because you're so eager to jump into selling and recruiting**? Are you in a position to throw away that kind of money?

I doubt it. That's why it's worth waiting until you are certain you know how to approach a contact before reaching out. Instead of immediately dialing that number as soon as you've organized your list, spend the rest of your time learning the ropes for contacting and scheduling calls.

DAY 5-7: FIRST CONTACT

For those eager to really jump into network marketing, those first four days can feel like they take forever. But as you round your way into the second half of the first week, you're finally ready to do some business! This is the moment you'll actually reach out to people, schedule some calls to discuss products and the opportunity, and hopefully see your first sales or enroll your first recruit.

- Familiarize yourself with the product and learn from top sellers.
- Start contacting warm contacts—three to five calls a day.
- Seek that first sale.

All that said, we're still going to move forward slowly and carefully. The first goal in these final days of week one is to spend time learning more about the product and to start looking into the top sellers for your company. If there are any materials available about their strategies or sales pitch, start reviewing those. You don't have to be at that level right away, but you want to *start learning from the best right now*.

As you continue to study, though, you can finally start to reach out to some of those contacts. Taking a page from those hairdressers I mentioned before—who move from cutting wigs to their friends' hair—you're going to begin by reaching out to those closest to you.

I recommend that the first ten people you contact should be **the ones you would really like to recruit and work with**. This is the hottest part of the list. Said another way, these aren't necessarily the coolest people you know or the ones you assume would have the most contacts. Instead, it's the people you'd want to go into business with because you like to be around them. This group includes **the people you're close to who you suspect are open to trying something new**.

We start here because, like those hairdressers, this group is going to be forgiving. They'll be okay if you don't know all the answers yet or if you stumble a bit in your presentation. They'll be willing to see what you're trying to say. They'll be patient, and they'll be forgiving. Consider this a chance to get some real-world training before heading out into the wild. Your future self will thank you.

Contacting and inviting is a so-called "gateway skill" in network marketing. It will determine if you can build a business or not. So it's extremely important to get some practice here and develop this skill early. In my own experience, I reached out to my best friend, Samuel; Sasha, whom I saw every day at the gym; my sister-in-law, Neuza; and my mother.

I know this can feel intimidating. Many people want to start at the opposite end of their list—with people who are almost strangers—because they're afraid to be embarrassed. If you can't get over this fear, it suggests you aren't fully convinced by this opportunity.

As we'll discuss in the next chapter, you have to believe this is an opportunity. You're doing them a favor by introducing these products!

Now, once you start reaching out, you have two clear options for what you're going to offer these people. You can try to sell them some of the product from the company. Or you can try to recruit them into the business.

We'll discuss strategy on this point more in the next chapter, but quickly, **I recommend beginning with sales**. If you love these products already, it's an easy and natural step to recommend them to people you care about. Likely, someone will take you up on your pitch, if for no other reason than they like you, trust you, and they're willing to take a chance on you.

And if some of them want to discuss joining your business already? Well, one of the coolest things about network marketing is that you get to decide who you work with. And signing a new subscriber from your closest friends and family in week one puts you way ahead of the rest of the pack.

ALL-STAR GOAL FOR WEEK ONE: HOSTING YOUR FIRST PRODUCT PRESENTATION

A product presentation is a fun event you can hold in your home. Just gather some friends, order a few pizzas, offer some drinks, and you can show off all the products from your company. This is an old, tried-and-true sales method that's been popular since the Avon Ladies and Tupperware Parties of the 1960s.

If you've completed everything else on your list, this is a great end-of-the-week goal where you can likely pick up a few sales—and maybe even some subscription interest.

YOU DON'T HAVE TO REINVENT THE WHEEL

When you start reaching out to your first contacts, keep in mind that you can rely on tried and true techniques for sales. You aren't the first person to call up a friend and try to sell them something. It's happened millions upon millions of times in network marketing (and in other forms of business as well, of course).

So *there's no need to overthink this*. Instead, I recommend picking up Eric Worre's *Go Pro* book. There, he breaks down the various *contacting and inviting strategies* that are most effective in this profession. Briefly, those are:

- Direct: Telling your prospective customer this product is for them.
- Indirect: Asking for advice on how to sell this great product.
- Super-Indirect: Telling the prospective customer the product isn't for them but someone they know.

I know this all sounds a little vague here, but Worre spells these ideas out in detail. Once you fully understand them, based on the relationship you have with this prospect, *you can decide which method you will use*.

The one additional idea I'd add to Worre's excellent sales advice is the idea of *"qualifying" your "lead."* What this means is that you have a conversation with the person you're trying to sell a product to (this is your "lead" in sales terminology). In this conversation, you can find out about their needs, wishes, and dreams. Then you can customize the invitation even better. The chances that a person accepts an invitation increases dramatically if they understand their unique advantage and benefits if they try it.

If you listen carefully, understand their need, and choose your words to suit that need…BINGO! You probably have a sale!

SLOW DOESN'T MEAN STOP

In this chapter, I've tried to emphasize the importance of going slow in this first week. But I don't want you to feel like I'm holding you back for no reason. My goal here is to make sure you don't burn through your contacts or burn yourself out before you even get going. After all, a poorly constructed rocket can blow up on the launch pad.

But there's a fine line between keeping a good pace and holding someone back. Unfortunately, that's just what some sponsors do. I know this personally. My own sponsor ended up quitting network marketing, so I ended up having to sponsor myself. I bought the product, read the right books, and started grinding on my own.

This may be the case for you. If you get through the first week and find that your sponsor hasn't provided you with all the information I recommend you review their onboarding process. If they aren't sharing all these tasks or helping you in any way for you to prepare for calls or sales (even after you request help), *you may have to face up to the fact that your sponsor won't be of any help to you on this journey*.

Importantly, that doesn't mean you should give up or leave the company you're working with! If you've done your due diligence, and you know this company has real products with real value that you are passionate about—if you know there's a real path forward and upward with your business—then there's no reason you should be the one to leave.

Instead, think of yourself as an entrepreneur whose chief supplier of materials sucks. If that happened in your business, you wouldn't just close up shop, would you? Instead, you'd keep your head down, work hard, keep the business growing, and look for an alternative supplier.

It's the same way in network marketing. ***If you work hard and see some results, your upline will take notice.*** And that's the best moment to reach out to someone further up the chain who can teach and coach you.

This is exactly what happened to me. Within a few weeks, I got a call from someone higher up in the company who'd noticed how impressive my numbers were. When I let them know that my sponsor was struggling to keep up with the pace of my development and ambitions, they stepped in and provided me with the guidance I wasn't getting elsewhere.

To get that attention, you have to strike a real balance between going methodically through the steps and showing eagerness in everything you do. I always notice when a new subscriber is hungry for this opportunity. If I give them two days to finish five tasks, they're done in four hours. When I check in on their progress, everything is well thought out and organized. When I say they have to wait to move forward, they dig into other material.

Once they start making calls, their passion shows through, and they get some strong early sales. That's the sort of person I want to reach out to directly and help make the most of their career.

I know that on some level, going at this speed can be frustrating when you are that eager. But the truth is, ***if you're following every step here, you're actually racing at an incredible speed***. You're accomplishing more in a week than most new network marketers do in three. In fact, you may go so fast that an inexperienced sponsor asks you to slow down!

If that happens to you, don't listen. Because you aren't going too slowly or too fast right now. You're going just at the right speed to build that rocket, hit escape velocity, and eventually land on the moon.

COUNTDOWN CHECKLIST

3. Be enthusiastic, but don't rush through your network marketing onboarding in your first few days.

2. Make a list of 150 contacts, but make sure you understand your company, their products, their sales material, and any selling advice before you start making calls.

1. Reach out to the ten people in your life you'd like to work with and who are most willing to hear what you're trying to say while you refine your sales pitch.

CHAPTER 5

WEEK 2: YOUR FIRST WINS

Let me tell you a story. I was a young network marketer just starting out in my new profession. Despite realizing the potential in this business, I wasn't sure if it was for me. It all sounded good—it looked right on paper—but there was a big gap between what was possible and what I could actually accomplish.

That first month was crucial for me. In my first few weeks, I sold $3,000 worth of perfume. I made 50 percent commission on that. So I made $1,500 in my first month.

Those early sales made all the difference. It's no exaggeration to say that if I hadn't done that, I wouldn't be here today, writing this book.

Those sales were crucial not just because they gave me confidence but because they gave me a story. I could go to a potential customer and say with complete accuracy that people loved this product. And I could go to a recruit and honestly tell them that they could be making thousands of dollars within a month.

This story has been so central to my time in network marketing, I still tell it on stage. I still use it with potential recruits.

If someone like me, with no experience in sales—who was, honestly, an awkward salesperson at the time—could sell $3,000 of product in one month, anyone can do it.

It's a simple story, but it's true and to the point, and it's won over countless people who were on the fence about network marketing.

—SANDRO

THE TWO PILLARS OF NETWORK MARKETING

As I mentioned briefly in the last chapter, there are two pillars through which you bring in revenue and grow your business in network marketing: sales and recruitment. Sales involves **selling the products of your company directly to customers**—at first those in your network and then more broadly. Recruitment is when you **sign someone up to start their own business that you sponsor**.

There are various perspectives within the network marketing community about which of these pillars you should concentrate your energy on. Sales can offer immediate revenue that continues for as long as your customer remains a customer. Longer term, recruitment can lead to exponential growth because you get a percentage of the profits from sales and additional recruiting from every recruit you sponsor. We'll discuss this further in the next chapter.

Personally, I believe in pursuing *a 50/50 split between sales and recruitment*. In the first place, you should always have your hand in sales. *Sharing your passion for the products and interesting new customers is fundamental to the network marketing model.* It's what distinguishes it from a pyramid scheme. A focus on sales proves that these products are valuable, useful, and attractive in their own right. Remember, you should only be involved with a company selling stuff you like to use and you want others to use!

Continuing to sell the product will also make you a better sponsor. As you know right now (but may forget a year or two down the line), one of the main areas a new recruit needs guidance on is selling the product. How can you guide your recruits through their first few sales if you stop selling regularly? And how can you inspire them to see the true value of those products if you aren't regularly sharing that information with customers?

This isn't just hypothetical to me. I still follow this advice. My organization has 170,000 members at this point, but I am still very much involved in selling the products of my company. I use them. I genuinely promote them in my network. And I am even involved with my sponsor company when it comes to testing new product options and giving feedback. The products remain a core part of what I'm doing.

For our purposes in week two, though, a focus on sales is crucial because it's simply *the easiest path to getting some "quick wins."* This is a term business leaders use to describe the easy successes they can achieve quickly to build up some momentum in their company. Quick wins are particularly important when starting a new business or bringing in a new leader, and they're particularly important in network marketing. The master of this field, Eric Worre, says that there's a proven formula for success in this profession. A new network marketer who generates just $2 in sales in the first two weeks will remain active for another ninety days. Those who fail to make that first sale usually lose interest.

To get some quick wins in network marketing, all you have to do is contact those 150 people you already know and speak to your experience with the products you've used. Whether you're talking to them one-on-one or in a group—whether it's over the phone, in person, or via text or email—just tell people how great these products are. If just one friend gives one product a try, you've made a sale!

And that's key in week two—because *your ultimate goal at the end of this week is to have made at least one sale*. That's the bare minimum requirement. Your real aim, though, is to *make back your entire investment so far in your company* and, hopefully, make a little profit.

Once you've hit these benchmarks, recruitment becomes much easier. With recruitment, you'll need to "pitch" your potential recruits. And while, as we'll see, your sponsor should do the heavy lifting on your first few efforts, you still need something to tell people that gets them interested in your business beyond the quality of the products. Essentially, what you need is a story.

TIME TO WRITE YOUR STORY

Those quick sales wins are so important for your business because moving into sponsorship requires you to develop your story. Recruitment is a heavier lift than just selling the product, and it's even heavier if you have yet to make a dollar in your business yourself.

Think about your sponsorship pitch to your contacts from their perspective. If you haven't made a dollar in the first month, how can you sell this business model as a life-changing opportunity to someone else? What do you say if they ask how much money you've made in the business so far?

Let's game this out. Imagine someone asking that second question. "This all sounds interesting. But how much have you made in this business?"

Of course, you want to answer something like, "I'm making $70,000 a month right now, and that amount is going up every month!" But you aren't there yet. You're still building your rocket; you aren't on the moon yet.

So instead, at this point in your journey, you have two options. You can either say something like, "Well, technically, I haven't made any money yet. But I'm sure it's going to start coming in any day."

Or you can say, "Well, I've only been doing this for two weeks. I spent $300 on subscription fees and products—which I love, by the way! And I've already made my money back and a small profit. So what do you have to lose by signing up?"

The second story is simply far more compelling. What do they have to lose? They get great products, the potential to make a lot of money, and at the very least, they'll make their money back in a couple weeks. What's not to like?

This is why your story is so important. In the future, you'll have the stories of people on your team and your own impressive financial success to build into an even more compelling story. In fact, you can probably revise this story in a matter of weeks once you've made some real money and perhaps even helped a recruit or two get off to a good start. But for now, this story is a good start! It should get your recruitment off the ground, and that's our main concern at the moment.

To develop your own story, you don't have to be a creative writer or great public speaker. This process doesn't require a ton of originality (although a little creativity in your storytelling won't hurt!). ***All you have to do is focus on the positive side of your experience so far in network marketing.***

This story is your "proof of concept," a term businesses use to describe the proof that a new product idea could really work if fully developed and produced. In our case, this means we can prove to people the thing we're selling (here, the products of the company and the business model of the company) works.

You can use the example above to build your own story, but feel free to expand a bit and make it your own. You can include extra benefits—maybe network marketing has given you a reason to reconnect with old friends or get out of the house more. Maybe you've used those first profits to start paying off a credit card bill that's been dragging down your finances for years or to get your kid a toy they've been begging for. These are all additional positive reasons a potential recruit might want to join you in going to the moon. So long as these anecdotes are true and come from a genuine place, they can show the potential of this business venture.

Just remember, you're not selling them your success; you're documenting it with facts so you can help them understand how network marketing can improve their lives. **The core of your story must have that proof of concept that proves to your audience that this business can, in fact, make money.**

BRINGING THE RIGHT ENERGY

Another reason we want some quick wins this week is because a lot of network marketing comes down to bringing positive, enthusiastic energy to your encounters. And that's really hard to maintain without a little early momentum.

Success leads to more success. The sooner you make a few sales, the sooner you feel more confident about your new business and the products you're selling. **And that confidence can be infectious!**

Just like with your story, think about this from the perspective of the person you're talking to. Do you want to buy something from someone quiet and uncertain who doesn't know much about the products they're selling or the business model they're recruiting for? Do you want to buy from someone who is desperate and aggressive, trying to push things off on you that you aren't even sure you want? Or do you want to meet with someone passionate, high energy, confident, and self-assured about what they're selling?

It's obviously the last one, right? **That's the sales "sweet spot": someone excited but not hyper, confident but not aggressive, certain but not cocky, knowledgeable but not a know-it-all.** Sometimes, the obvious advice is correct: treat others as you would want to be treated. Be authentic, considerate of people's time, and focused on the value of this opportunity from their perspective.

I speak from experience here. When I was first contacted by network marketers as a young IT entrepreneur, I often felt they were trying to sell me on a project they didn't fully understand themselves. It seemed like they just wanted me to join so I could do all the work for them. In a word, it felt inauthentic, perhaps even at times deceptive.

That's why those first sales are so important. You can speak from a place of authenticity. You can feel the potential of this business model in your bones, and that allows you to speak from experience and to authentically see where this business can take you. You don't have to get this pitch perfect right away, but you should always be aiming for it—and getting closer with each interaction.

DAY 8–10: GET THAT FIRST SALE

Week 2's mission is to make those early sales and build toward your first new recruit. If you've already made those sales, great work! Keep going and don't lose momentum while you continue to follow the process. But if you haven't made a sale at the start of the week, don't worry. These first few days of the week are dedicated to changing that.

Continue to make calls to those on your list, working your way down from those warmest connections to the coldest. At the same time, work with your sponsor, apply their advice, and do the homework. Keep using the products and researching your company. This should all help you improve how you talk about the products you're offering your connections.

- Complete any remaining Week 1 tasks.
- Organize your first home presentation.
- Do a product knowledge deep dive and keep learning from top sellers.
- Follow up with initial contacts and book another conversation.
- Learn about addressing skepticism and answer contact objections.
- Offer product trials.
- Start crafting your story.

First and foremost, if you haven't completed all the tasks from Week 1, stop what you're doing and finish those before progressing to Week 2. Assuming you're caught up, now is a good time to have that first at-home product presentation if you didn't get to it last week. As I mentioned before, that's a great opportunity to get your first sale (or even your first few sales).

This is also a good moment to really dive deeply into the products your company has to offer. If you placed your order at the beginning of Week 1, you should have had your company's products for a few days at this point. ***If you haven't already, start using them, learning about what makes them stand out, and getting more passionate about them.*** If you only entered network marketing because you want to make quick money—if you don't care about the products you sell—then it's really hard to convince people to take a chance on those products or join your company.

You don't have to be a master salesperson to be a success in network marketing, but you do have to be authentic, honest, and trustworthy. In the future, you will be able to point to many examples of people who use these products who are part of your organization, but for now, you are your only example. If you ask people to use the products but you don't use them, why would anyone try them out? **You have to believe in these products first. That passion will help others do the same.**

While you continue working your way down your contact list, you should also start recontacting those contacts who showed interest in buying products or joining your business already. You don't need to constantly blow up their phones pushing for a sale, but if you've explained the value of the products and perhaps mentioned the business opportunity you're pursuing and they've shown interest, **there's no harm following up to see if they're still interested**.

I know there's concern about annoying those you care about most—potentially even burning some valuable relationships. But you can avoid that by focusing on this experience from their perspective. You've chosen your company wisely, you love these products, and you just want to share them. Why wouldn't you reach out again to see if they want to try them for themselves?

Let's think about this in a different way. Imagine you'd just tried acupuncture for your chronic back pain, and miraculously, you're pain-free for the first time in years. What would you do next? You'd tell everyone you know that they should try it too, right? After all, **you're really doing them a favor by pointing them in that direction.**

Now, let's say you talked to one friend who has been struggling with knee pain after a running injury. They're interested in trying acupuncture, but they wanted a few days to think about it. What would you do after that conversation? I think it's the most natural thing in the world to contact them again a few days later and, along with catching up on each other's lives, ask if they've given acupuncture any more thought. Do they have any questions about it? Do they want you to speak to your acupuncturist and help them set up an appointment?

In this case, you aren't harassing them or annoying them. **You're presenting them with an opportunity.** And once again, you shouldn't make this decision for them. If you go to the ten people who love you best and you believe in the product/service/system, the odds are someone from that list will take a chance on this with you—even if it takes a couple more calls.

And even if they don't, you've done no harm. You've simply shared an opportunity with them that you thought would genuinely do them some good. And who knows? Like my sister-in-law, they may change their mind later.

As you continue to contact people and follow up, you're bound to deal with some pretty common objections that arise in network marketing. Your company will probably have information on dealing with these objections. You should study those now. And if you want another resource, I've included a list of objections and some powerful responses in the back of the book. Read through those and then practice delivering them. Trust me, once you get started, **the same objections will come up over and over, and the sooner you become comfortable fielding and responding to those questions, the better.**

As the week goes on, if your company allows it, you can start getting some additional quick wins through product trials. This is a great way to convince people who are on the fence about trying these products out. ***Even if you're making just a small profit on these first sales, you're still improving your story as you go.***

By midweek, you should hopefully have made enough sales that you can start drafting your story. You can improve your storytelling technique by using any of your company's materials on writing or practicing your story.

DAY 11–14: PITCH AND RECRUIT

I've kept the list for the second half of this week short because this is an important moment in your network marketing business. During these days, you want to keep building on your sales knowledge and keep increasing your sales, but simultaneously ***it's now time to pivot to recruitment.***

Continue calling contacts, following up, and increasing sales.

Sign up one or two recruits.

On this first point, you just have to keep doing more of what you're already doing. Work your way down your list, following up with those who show interest, answering their questions, and trying to add more sales.

But now you're also going to offer them a second opportunity. If they're ready, they can go into business for themselves, build their own rocket, and get to the moon. This is where your story really comes into play. Once you've made a few sales, you can start presenting this opportunity to others. It's already working for you. You've already made your money back; it could do the same for them!

You can present this opportunity to every person on your contact list. In fact, it makes sense to go back to the top and reach back out to those who have already shown some interest. If they bought some products, ask if they like them. And if they do, would they be interested in doing what you're doing?

However, I'm going to once again pump the brakes on you, just a little. For these first few pitches, **I highly recommend you do them with your sponsor or upline manager.** The first few times, your job is just to connect the interested party with your sponsor. That way, you can watch an experienced network marketer make the pitch and explain the business model. The reason to bring your sponsor in is that there's still a lot you don't know about the company, the products, and network marketing in general. And that's okay! You aren't expected to be an expert at this point. This also allows you to bring in an experienced third-party perspective that can increase your credibility and the professionalism of the project.

Proactively ask for their help pitching the business. Once you've seen it done a few times, you can start taking it on yourself. And with your sponsor's help, you should be able to sign a recruit by the end of the week.

ALL-STAR GOAL FOR THE WEEK: YOUR FIRST SOCIAL MEDIA POST

It's hard to run a network marketing business these days without social media. But that doesn't mean you have to start using it immediately. I didn't touch my social media accounts for my entire first year. At this point, it's still a luxury. But if you are a regular social media user or feel ambitious enough to set up an account, the end of Week 2 is a great time to make that first post about your new business.

When you do, though, be thoughtful about what you post. It can be tempting to go out and make a splashy sales pitch to all your followers, trying to gin up some extra sales. But this kind of aggressive selling often backfires. Instead of seeing sales, you'll see people unfollowing you or putting your account on mute.

Instead, this first post should just show your authentic excitement about your new business. You could share your success, talking about how happy you are to have made five sales in just two weeks. Or take a photo with your first recruit. You can mention how you aren't just changing your own life but helping change someone else's too.

The key here is being honest and authentic while giving a positive impression of the business and its products. Leave the aggressive selling to the influencers.

MAINTAIN CONTACT

Before we move on, I want to take a quick moment to speak about communication. Throughout this second week, you're going to spend a lot of time on the phone and emailing. Not only are you contacting people on your list and following up with those who show interest, *you should also be in daily contact with your sponsor*.

This is true even if they aren't that helpful or communicative themselves. Remember, you can show the entire upline how ambitious and eager you are, whether your sponsor helps you or not.

This contact doesn't have to be extensive. But if you have a question, send them a text. Or just send them an email update at the end of each day with the details of the number of people you've contacted and any sales you've made.

As these examples suggest, texts and emails are fine, but I think a short phone call is often best. A quick fifteen-minute recap can keep your sponsor in the loop, get you some valuable advice, show your eagerness to succeed in this business, and keep you motivated to keep going.

COUNTDOWN CHECKLIST

3. Focus on getting a few "quick wins" through sales with your hottest contacts.

2. After you've made your money back, write the first version of your story to share with potential recruits.

1. Reach out to your contacts and start recruiting with the help of your sponsor.

CHAPTER 6

WEEK 3: THE TRANSITION TO ENTREPRENEURIAL SUCCESS

Sandro's story is really about the power of commitment.

Sandro told me about his first reaction when he received his proposal to enter network marketing. His response was clear: "Do you think I'm someone who goes around selling perfumes?"

A few days later, though, on a Zoom call with his manager, he witnessed a reality he had never imagined: hundreds of consultants, a thriving organization, and an opportunity that went far beyond mere sales. In that moment, he later told me, something inside him clicked. He decided he was all in.

And once he made that commitment, everything changed. Sandro dove in completely: daily Zoom calls, books devoured with a hunger for knowledge, questions upon questions to understand every gear of the business. In just two weeks, he had already grasped all the connections of this profession.

In just four months, he reached the Diamond qualification, breaking all company records in Europe. But it wasn't just about titles. Sandro was already building a new way of doing network marketing, one that would turn it into a real, globally-recognized entrepreneurial business.

I met him right at that moment, four months after his entry. I saw him and immediately understood he was not an ordinary person. His dedication was unmatched. He was already a success, but he was just getting started. I told him, "You will be the future of this company." And I was right.

In just four years, Sandro led the company to the top of the European market, becoming a leader in the fast-moving consumer goods sector. Along with the leadership at his company, he created one of the strongest communities in the world, with a clear vision: to build something that lasts over time, forms leaders, and gives people the chance to radically change their lives.

I remember the precise moment we decided to develop our academy together. We were on a trip, and Sandro looked at me and asked, "Do you think, Denis, that we are capable of building this thing for our community?"

My answer was immediate: "Absolutely yes, Sandro."

And from that day, our academy was no longer a dream: it was a reality. Once Sandro was committed, I knew it would get done.

This is Sandro's strength: seeing what doesn't yet exist and having the courage, determination, and vision to make it real.

His journey is proof that, with the right mindset and total commitment, there are no limits.

—DENIS

TIME TO RECOMMIT

If you've made it this far in network marketing, the first thing I want you to do is give yourself a round of applause. In my experience, more than 80 percent of those who enter this profession drop out by this point. While the numbers are better in my organization—using this method—it's still a huge accomplishment to have the motivation and dedication to make the kind of real, concrete investments in your own business that you have already. You're well on your way now to becoming a network marketing professional—and changing your life forever.

With that said, it might seem odd that this is the moment I'm recommending you really commit. I know, you've already committed multiple times to this enterprise: when you signed up with your network marketing company, when you started to reach out to your contacts, and when you made that first sale. But in Week 3 you have to recommit again because **what you're about to embark on is building a completely new business**.

Let me explain. Up until now, you've mostly been building a direct sales business. You reach out to people, explain how great these products are, and make a few sales. Maybe you have one or two friends who have signed up to help you sell more.

That's a great start, and it can lead to a nice little side income. But from here on out, you're trying to build something bigger, more lucrative, and more sustainable. **If you want real income that continues to grow for months and years to come, you need to recruit more people.**

You can think about the change like this. Robert Kiyosaki, the author of *Rich Dad Poor Dad*, breaks down our ways of making money into a "cashflow quadrant" with four possibilities. There are employees, self-employed individuals, business owners, and investors. Right now, after two weeks, you are on a trajectory that will eventually allow you to make the switch from an employee to self-employed. That's a life-changing shift, and for some, that's all they're looking for. If that's all you want, then congratulations! You probably don't need much of the rest of this book. Just keep making calls, building a client list, and recruiting a friend here or there to help you. Plenty of network marketers remain self-employed and either make a little money on the side or make a respectable income doing sales with a small team of friends.

But there's a downside to this decision. Being self-employed means **the only way you can sustain your income is by doing all the sales work yourself.** If you want more than that, you need to become an entrepreneur, which, again, means you have to bring more recruits into your business.

Entrepreneurship is where network marketing shows you its real power. **This is where you can turbocharge your income and turn into a huge, successful business.** To do that requires more work and commitment, hence your need to sit down and make a firm decision on just how far you want to take this.

When I talk to new recruits at this point in their journey, I recommend that they hold off recommitting immediately. I don't want them to impulsively agree or back out based on how they're feeling in that moment. So I give them forty-eight hours to really think this through. After that, I ask them to make their decision: is this a business or are you going to do all the work yourself?

ADDING THE ENGINE

Once you're truly committed to taking the next step with your business, it's time to start getting more ambitious this week. Entrepreneurship is driven by goals, motivation, and vision. Reaching your ultimate goal may take years. That means it may be years before you can take a long break and years before you can look away for a while and still expect income to keep coming in. This is why you shouldn't look at network marketing as the traditional get-rich-quick scheme. ***It's either a direct selling system or a means of real entrepreneurship, with all the expected work and sacrifices.***

It's also entrepreneurship with all its potential—and, let me remind you, without all the financial risk. There's no need to take out a budget-breaking loan here. It all comes down to how hard you work and how seriously you commit.

To think of this another way, up until now, we've been building our rocket by assembling the cargo bay, the flight deck, and the wings. Now, these pieces can be used to reach the moon, but they could also be turned into the components of a jet without too much work. In other words, they could turn into a machine that gets you airborne but keeps you within the earth's atmosphere.

To achieve the sort of liftoff that breaks free of the earth's gravitational pull, you're going to need to strap on some booster rockets. That's what will take you from the modest success of a few sales and a couple recruits to the kind of entrepreneurial success you've been dreaming of.

To see just how this next stage really explodes your potential, we can do some simple math. This is the same formula I first encountered in *The 45-Second Presentation That Will Change Your Life* by Don Failla when I was beginning my own journey.

When I present this idea to recruits on my own team, I always start with a basic premise. My network marketing company sells lots of high-end toiletries and personal care products. So I ask these new recruits how many people do they know who regularly use some sort of fragrance. It could be perfume, cologne, whatever. How many use *something*?

The answer is, of course, everyone. And that's the same answer to my second question: how many people do they know who would like to have a second source of income?

Now, here's the power of network marketing in action. If you share your passion for the products of your company with all your contacts, how many do you think will buy something—just to give it a try? And if you share the potential for that second income, how many will join you?

Probably at least a few, right? And that's all you actually need to get started in network marketing! ***All you need for this math to work is five people who want to sign up and try this business model out.*** Once you have five people selling products along with you, they can reach out to their 150 contacts. If each of them brings in five new recruits, all the sudden your network has jumped in size to twenty-five people.

$$5 \times 5 = 25$$

From there, those recruits can add five more new team members.

$$25 \times 5 = 125$$

And before you know it, that line will add five more of their own.

$$125 \times 5 = 625$$

When you add all those people together, you now have a really serious team.

$$625 + 125 + 25 + 5 = 780$$

Remember, to reach that number *all you need is for each person to bring in five people on their own.* No one has to do more than that for your business to reach that size. And if each one of these recruits sells just five products, we're now talking about moving serious numbers.

$$780 \text{ distributors} \times 5 = 3{,}900$$

We can then add each recruit back in because everyone on your team should also be a customer.

$$3900 + 780 = 4{,}680$$

By the time you really build this business out, then, you could be moving 4,680 products every month. At my company, the average price for a bottle of perfume is $30. So someone in my organization with this setup would sell $140,400 worth of product.

$$4680 \times 30 = 140{,}400$$

That would lead to between $12,000 and $14,000 a month for the person who built this business!

This is possible from just working within your own connections and encouraging each recruit to do the same.

Also, keep in mind, these are conservative numbers. As I'll lay out in a moment, you can almost certainly sign up more than five people from that initial list. And there's no reason you can't sign up more as you expand your connections.

In fact, the longer-term direction these numbers point to is often hard to even imagine at the start. But the numbers aren't lying. This is mathematics, not opinion. This approach creates a domino effect with truly life-changing potential.

Now, you won't achieve this result in one week. Or one month. But I have seen plenty of people do it in nine to twelve months. And if you stick with this book, you'll be on the path to achieving it within that timeframe yourself.

CONTINUE TO RELY ON YOUR UPLINE

The name of the game for this week and next, then, is recruitment. That doesn't mean you stop doing sales—quite the contrary, that's a key part of your business and often the access point for recruitment anyway. We'll talk about this more in the next chapter. Stick with recruiting for now. As you recruit, I want to once again briefly pump the brakes on one crucial part of this process: presentations. Some of you are going to be ambitious enough that you want to take over presenting the business model yourself and even onboarding new recruits who sign up. **But you're still in the learning phase in Week 3, and I highly recommend you leave this work to your sponsor and upline.**

Someone within your company should still be offering to do this for you at this point, and you should definitely take them up on that offer. The process of presenting the business is simply too complex and risky to handle without more experience. **If your recruit asks one question that you can't answer, it's over.** People respond to confidence, certainty, and expertise. You are expected to have a certain level of knowledge and experience that you can transmit in that really important first meeting.

If your sponsor isn't willing to keep doing these presentations, you need to connect with someone higher up your upline. **Don't be afraid to reach out!** I love when this happens in my organization because it shows the people who really believe in this. It can also present some really cool opportunities.

For instance, I was recently in Zurich, meeting a couple that a recruit in my organization wanted me to speak to. This couple were the owners of the most expensive jewelry shop on the most expensive street in Zurich, which is one of the most expensive cities in the world. Needless to say, these people would be great recruits. But as soon as I mentioned network marketing, the wife made a face. Her mother had been involved in a network marketing company years before, and it had turned out to be a scam. She was still upset about the whole thing. There was no way she was going to join a network company herself.

Luckily, I knew how to handle that kind of response. I've talked to skeptical entrepreneurs many times, and I know the approach that works best to convince them to give this opportunity another chance.

"Listen," I told her. "I hear you. This is clearly not for you, but maybe you know someone who might be interested. Let me explain how this works in a little more detail."

Instead of focusing on our companies' products like I might with some other prospects, I explained to her that network marketing is just a business model—it's just another way to sell products. I made the case I've made to you here, that this is just a business strategy that allows a company to sell their products without having to cover expenses like rent and employees or make a deal with a large distributor. As an entrepreneur herself, she could see the value of that perspective. In fact, not only did she see the value of it, she was interested in setting up her own network marketing company for her jewelry business! She even went so far as passing along some of her contacts she thought would be a good match for the business.

Again, this was not the right presentation for everyone, but I've done this so many times, I can read what argument works best and know how to present it to each prospect.

This process takes practice and mastery. And that means continuing to watch those who have mastered it. Seeing these presentations over and over again allows you to absorb all the questions that come up, all the possible answers, and all the methods of sharing information for various prospects.

Besides, at this point, you should be focusing on contacting people on your list, selling products, and recruiting. You don't need something else to worry about. Just watch others perform and learn by watching.

DAY 15-17: SCALING AND ORGANIZING

Once someone truly commits to the entrepreneurship path, everything in Weeks 3 and 4 builds toward a single goal: to achieve Core Rank at their organization. *Core Rank is the level where you start making money that feels real and substantial.* Depending on the company you work with, Core Rank usually means you're bringing in $400 to $500 in commission. It's usually achievable within a month or two.

To reach that level, we need to keep the list short and focused on building your team.

- Plot your path to Core Rank.
- Help guide your recruits into the onboarding process.

Crucially, **Core Rank is a team goal.** Technically, in some companies, you could do this simply through your own sales, but for this to really be a sustainable business that allows you to make significant income, you need to be building a team to help you.

To plot your path to Core Rank, you'll have to do a little math. First, look at how much revenue/income is required to achieve this rank with your company. Then find out the monthly average sales revenue brought in by your colleagues in your area. Your sponsor should be able to tell you this number.

From there, it's all a matter of dividing that total number by the average to figure out how many new recruits you need to add to your team over the next two weeks.

Let's say that you do this math, and to achieve Core Rank, you need seventeen people making average sales numbers for a month. Now, it'd be nice if you could recruit and onboard all these people yourself. But that's simply too much for most people, particularly this early on. So your aim should be lower—somewhere around ten people. You can then help those ten people add seven more recruits themselves—getting their businesses off the ground.

Most people can find at least ten potential recruits from among their 150 contacts. This isn't opinion; once again, it's pretty basic math. Let's say, of those 150, only seventy-five are interested—that's a low bar when you're offering a second source of income selling quality products to your friends. Of those, maybe only sixty will show up for the three-way presentation call you schedule with your sponsor. The average conversion rate is about 20 percent for people who attend one of those presentations. That would give you twelve new recruits! Even if two of those people get cold feet, you'd still have enough to achieve your team goal!

And even if three of those twelve didn't sign up, no problem. You just need to help your new recruits add one additional new member of the team. **With these numbers, all each new recruit needs to do is make an average number of sales and recruit one person—at most.** And most likely, at least one person among those ten will want to shoot for the moon like you and will overachieve.

Once you sign new recruits, though, you can't just abandon them. We'll talk about this more in the next chapter, but make sure each person gets your attention, and you are there to help them as much as they need through those early stages. While your sponsor should still probably be doing the bulk of the onboarding, remember that you are your recruit's first contact. You need to be responsive and provide as much guidance, advice, and support as possible.

Stepping in to provide this support is easier than you might think. To begin with, you can point them to this book and the exact same process you've begun following to success. You may not yet be an expert on every aspect of network marketing, but you've been through this process up to this point and can support new members as they take their first steps into this opportunity.

DAY 18–21: STAY THE COURSE

The remaining tasks for this week could not be more straightforward. As you continue to wind your way through the last names on your contact list, you should also:

- Keep following up with hesitant prospects.
- Ensure your new recruits are doing the same.
- Reconnect with your real goals.

Essentially, *all you need to do is reach out to new people, check in on those who are considering purchasing some product or joining your team, and make sure all those you signed up who have completed their onboarding do the same*.

The only other activity you should complete this week is to review the goals you set for yourself in this business back in Week 1. Importantly, if they aren't already, **these should be concrete, real, personal goals**. This takes a little imagination sometimes.

As I mentioned in Week 1, so often, people just have a number in mind when they set their goals. Or they have a goal but don't know how much they need to achieve it. At times, people even just set sights on a rank without connecting it to their lives at all!

I was recently in Dubai and asked a group of managers what their short-, medium-, and long-term goals were. They all wrote down the same thing: each goal corresponded to a rank in our company.

But those weren't their *real* goals. Why did they want to achieve a certain rank? Why did they want to make $10,000 a month? What did they want their life to look like when they made that money?

$10,000 a month can pay for a lot of dreams. It can buy you a house or apartment almost anywhere in the world. It can cover travel to any country. Very quickly, you could pay off any debt—whether it's yours or your spouse's or your parents'. Whatever your dream, set a clear goal and then attach a number to it. Then work backward to the rank you need to reach.

In business, this is often called "finding your why"—a term coined by the author Simon Sinek—and *it's a crucial tool to maintain your motivation* as you build, grow, and maintain your business.

ALL-STAR GOAL FOR THE WEEK: CREATE YOUR OWN MATERIALS

In the previous week, you developed your own story. Now that you are pitching your experience to potential customers and recruits, you may need to start creating your own presentations that tell that story and explain the value of the products and opportunities you're offering. This was certainly true for me. When I joined my company, they had very limited content to work with, so I had to develop my own to fill in the gaps. If you are working with a relatively new company, this may be your experience as well.

Your presentation should follow a very simple structure:

1. Telling Your Story

2. Presenting Your Team/Community

3. Presenting Your Company

4. Business and Income Opportunities

5. Testimonials

If you follow this basic structure, you'll provide potential recruits with all the information they need in a neat, easy-to-follow presentation designed to increase their interest.

Of course, if your company has these materials already, it's perfectly fine to rely on them when discussing the business model and product. But if nothing else, you can start mapping this book's process onto the process and materials your company provides.

BECOMING A LEADER

Week 3 is a transition period. Before you were learning the basics; now you're learning more advanced skills (like the presentations you keep watching). Before you were running a direct sales business; now you're building an entrepreneurial business.

Part of that transition involves **embracing your role as a leader**. Leadership is such a huge topic that it would require a whole second book to really dig into. But this is a good moment to start becoming familiar with a few basic concepts.

In particular, if you are going to run a business with lots of recruits, you have to realize that you are a leader—**you're the model they will base their behavior and expectations off of**. So you have to consciously recognize that you are an example to others now. **Anything you expect others to do, you have to do it first.** And you have to be consistent. People tend to do what you do, not what you tell them to do.

And even that is only partly true. Frazer Brookes likes to say that people are going to do 50 percent of what you do and 100 percent of what you don't do. So be sure to display all the behaviors you want to see others show as they train, sell, and recruit on their own.

COUNTDOWN CHECKLIST

3. Recommit to growing an entrepreneurial business before turning your focus to recruitment.

2. Do the math to find the number of recruits you need to reach Core Rank in your company.

1. Recognize your position as a leader and lead by example.

WEEK 4: TRANSITION TO LEADERSHIP

Before I joined Sandro's organization, I was part of another network. I never really moved up there—not because I lacked the will but because something essential was missing: true leadership, a clear system, and mentoring that truly fit me.

I needed guidance. I needed a mentor who could provide clarity about the system and give me structure—someone who believed in me and showed me the path to success. What I had was a sponsor who constantly put pressure on me to somehow figure it all out myself.

Luckily, Sandro came along before I gave up. We connected on Instagram, and after the very first Zoom call I knew I had found where I belonged.

From the very beginning, he was so much more than a sponsor; he was a leader with heart—the mentor I'd been seeking. Thanks to Sandro, for the first time, I had a clear goal in mind: to reach the Core Rank quickly while building a team with the structure and passion in place for each new member to succeed as well.

Suddenly, I had a system. The path became tangible. I could progress step by step and could then lead my team up the same steps.

In just three weeks I reached the Core Rank, and within the first three months, I achieved three consecutive double rank-ups.

To this day, I remain deeply grateful to be part of this wonderful community, and I am excited for everything that's still to come.

—Irina

CONCRETE PROOF OF YOUR SUCCESS

Weeks 3 and 4 are really part of a single process. Indeed, depending on the number of hours you commit to your business each week and your rate or success, this may actually extend further. **Many network marketers end up taking six or seven weeks to achieve Core Rank**, which is our ultimate goal at the end of this first month. If that's you, don't worry. Even if it takes you a little longer, you're on course to assemble this rocket ship and take off for the moon.

Your focus is on Core Rank because your ultimate aim should be to enjoy the concrete results of all the work you're putting in. **Achieving Core Rank proves to you—and to your team— that this is a real business.** You've put in the tough hours of study, hit the pavement and reached out to hundreds of people, sold and recruited nonstop. Now, it's time to see that it was all worth it.

So this week, like Week 3, is about getting closer to that goal.

DAY 22-24: EXPAND AND RETAIN

Everything this week is just one more step you can take toward that ultimate goal for this first month: Core Rank. As we approach that end point, all your tasks should feed into that effort.

- Track progress for each member of the team on the path to Core Rank.
- Provide full support to your recruits.

This is the time to hit the road, knock on doors, make calls, emails, set up meetings, and schedule presentations with your sponsor. *The harder you go, the faster you move, the more you can build momentum.* And that's what you can then coast on to reach your Core Rank target.

To make sure you're on track to do that, build on the math you did in Week 3 and track your progress. How many of those seventeen recruits do you have on your team now? How many have been able to reach the sales figure you set for each of them?

This should help you to not just track your progress but see where some recruits might need a little extra help. If one recruit is now two weeks into their network marketing journey and hasn't made a sale, schedule some time with them to discuss the issues they're having. Perhaps they are struggling to write their story, so call them up and give them some pointers.

As you do this, *always try to put your own goals in the back of your mind and focus on the needs and desires of the person in front of you*. This is another part of the journey to becoming a leader that you started last week.

This view is crucial across every aspect of network marketing success. You should never focus on your sales or recruitment approach around how this helps you build your business. Instead, focus on how the person you're talking to sees these things. In other words, **to support those who are considering a sale or those who are joining your company, you have to see things from their perspective**. This requires developing new skills. **You have to listen more and listen better.** Listen not just to what the person you're talking to says but what their underlying concern is. What are they really trying to communicate to you?

When a new person starts in network marketing, it's far too common for the sponsor to just hand over a bunch of materials, send a few links, and then tell the new recruit to call if they have questions. Maybe this was your experience too. But if you want to make this business work, you should approach this a different way: **be supportive, attentive, and professional**.

Get to know the person you've recruited—even if you already do know them quite well. Why did they join? What appealed to them about the opportunity? What are their goals? What are their dreams? What skills do they bring? What do they need to work on?

Your job is to guide them toward their goals, not yours. You want them to get to their destination on the moon, not yours.

Remember, this person isn't a get-rich-quick opportunity.

They're a business partner that you might work with for the next fifteen to twenty years! They may also be—or soon become—a real friend. Because network marketing brings together people with a shared mission, passion, and goal, it often leads to many wonderful new connections.

In one way or another, then, this person may be important to you for many years to come. So give this person the sense that they are on the right team with the right sponsor.

DAY 25–28: LOOKING AHEAD

This is the final stretch of your first month, and ideally, your Core Rank goal should be in sight. Your aim here is to finish strong while also building more of the foundation that will allow your business to continue to thrive after the first month has passed.

- Make contact with any remaining people on your list.
- Seek feedback and grow some thicker skin.
- Celebrate all achievements so far.

At this point, you should be reaching the very bottom of your list of 150 people. That means you've discussed the products you're selling and the opportunities that come with network marketing with almost everyone you regularly encounter. That's a lot of experience, and it's now a good time to **review what you've learned from those interactions**. When things went wrong with a prospect, what caused the conversation to go off the rails? Did you give a mediocre answer? Did you fumble your presentation of the product? Did you call them late in the evening or show up late for lunch? Did you come across as nervous instead of confident?

Up to this point, I haven't mentioned the need to seek out and absorb feedback because in this first month, it's all about building momentum and getting the foundations down for your business. Letting too much criticism in early can erode your confidence just when you need to ramp it up. But now, you should be closing in on Core Rank with enough proof to show that you really can do this.

If you want to continue to grow your income and business, you need to get better. And that requires feedback. Unfortunately, some of that is going to be negative. But there's no reason to ignore it just for that reason.

As you take on more of the process yourself going forward, you have to be open to hearing ways you can improve. Sometimes, the thing we need to hear most is the hardest. **You're just starting out, and there's almost certainly some serious critiques of your technique as a seller, recruiter, and leader you need to absorb.** Most people want to fight back or shut out any criticism they receive, but to improve, you have to recognize that feedback is a gift! It allows you to see where your weaknesses are, which allows you to make them your strengths.

This isn't just a time for self-improvement, though. It's also a time to celebrate! **As you close in and eventually achieve Core Rank, you should be celebrating wins across your team.** And that means celebrating their wins as much as yours. Core Rank is an achievement you will reach together, and each new sale or recruit is a win for someone within your organization.

You need to celebrate for three key reasons. First, everyone likes a party, and celebrating keeps everyone feeling positive and motivated. It shows you're all going in the right direction together.

Second, there's an old business saying, "Celebrate everything you want to replicate." If your team will only replicate 50 percent of the behavior you model—as we discussed in the last chapter—*celebrating can encourage some additional positive behaviors across the whole team.* If one of your recruits goes out and signs up four people in a week, celebrate that! If another recruit smashes your weekly sales record, party on! These celebrations will encourage everyone to reach for those same goals.

Finally, celebrating together reminds everyone—including you—that everyone is working together for success. No one is in this to get rich off the backs of other people's work. ***This is a team of people building their own businesses. Everyone is heading to the moon together.***

These celebrations can range in size and scale depending on the nature of the achievement. Hitting Core Rank may be a pizza party-worthy event. Someone getting their first recruit might just earn a shout out in your team's WhatsApp group. Use your own discretion, but make sure people feel appreciated and they know what kind of behaviors earn those plaudits.

PAST THE POINT OF NO RETURN

Once you achieve Core Rank—whether it takes three weeks or eight—you should take a moment to appreciate how far you've come. After all, for most network marketers, this is the point of no return: **the moment they realize this could really, truly turn into a business, a career, and a lifestyle**.

Up until now, you've probably enjoyed a few positive benefits as you assemble your rocket. You might be selling and recruiting enough to make $100, $200, or even $300 a month. That's not nothing. But in the end, it's just a nice extra bonus to supplement your real income.

But as I mentioned already, Core Rank for most network marketing companies translates to around $500 a month. That's $6,000 a year—a substantial amount of money. That's enough to cover a really wonderful vacation for your whole family or to cover all your costs to eat out for a year.

You can think of this as the moment you step into the rocket and lock the door behind you. You aren't yet blasting off, but takeoff is about to commence. You're now ready for space travel.

From here on out, you have all the tools you need to become a successful network marketing entrepreneur. It's absolutely possible from this moment forward to keep doing what you've already learned while increasingly taking on those responsibilities you were previously handing off to your sponsor. When you're comfortable, you can start presenting the business and onboarding new members of your team.

You can just keep doing this forever and achieve growth over time. *The one thing you can't do at this point is sit back and expect the business to take care of itself.* As I've mentioned many times now, the key to true network marketing success is seeing this opportunity not as a get-rich-quick scheme but as a true business. That means you don't finish this first month and expect the cash to start pouring in. You immediately start building on what you've already created.

To further enhance this growth, you can begin setting monthly goals you and your team can achieve. Set the objective, figure out how many people you need in your team and how many sales they need to make, and motivate everyone to hit those targets. Then celebrate every time you pull it off!

As you set these targets, ***don't underestimate how important sales will continue to be for your business***. The argument against network marketing is that it's all about recruitment. The product is just an excuse to justify a pyramid scheme. But you've chosen to work with a legitimate business with products you care about and use. You should want to sell them and share them and use them. And that same philosophy should trickle down to your whole team.

The ideal balance for a network marketing business is 50 percent focus on sales and 50 percent on recruitment. You and everyone else in your organization should aim to strike that every week and every month.

You have to lead the way on this balance. Think of yourself as a new stamp that will be used to make new coins. If the stamp has imperfections, every coin will have those same imperfections. The only way to make good copies is to have a great stamp.

To truly stamp this perspective—and other positive behaviors—onto your team, you will need to increasingly take a lead role in onboarding your recruits. ***Going forward, you are going to play the role your sponsor has played for you.*** As the leader of this new organization, you have a responsibility for each person you recruit—and each person they recruit. ***It's your job now to make sure the people you've brought in have the same chance you have had. You can lead them to Core Rank!***

And with that last point made, you now have a complete blueprint to build your network marketing rocket ship in one month. In some sense, if you're comfortable continuing to see the kind of growth you're experiencing in this first month, you can probably put this book down—or at least skip to the final part. Just keep doing what you're doing.

But if you want to achieve something more incredible—if you really want to shoot off for the moon—in the next part of this book, I'll introduce the most powerful scaling strategy in all of network marketing: the 90-Day Run.

Be warned, though. This will be an intense process. If you aren't able to commit everything to scaling your business for ninety days, it's best to keep using the tools you already have for a while.

When you are ready, though, this is the strategy that can take your rocket and ensure it doesn't just get off the ground, but it breaks the sound barrier as it shoots off beyond the atmosphere. Stated another way, right now you've got standard rockets on your spaceship. The 90-Day Run is when we add the boosters that ensure we make it out of orbit.

COUNTDOWN CHECKLIST

3. Track your progress so you stay on track to reach Core Rank.

2. Celebrate your wins and the wins of members of your team.

1. Keep building on this progress each month until you're ready to complete your first 90-Day Run.

PART III

INJECTING THE ROCKET FUEL

CHAPTER 8

PREPARING FOR YOUR 90-DAY RUN

When I started in network marketing, I was full of curiosity—and full of doubts. I didn't know what to expect, but I knew one thing: I wanted more from life. I had a feeling that network marketing could provide that for me, but it felt like such a huge mountain to climb to get from where I was to where I wanted to be.

Then came the moment that changed everything. Sandro gathered his team together and announced we'd be going on a 90-Day Run.

The concept was simple and, at the same time, radical. For ninety days, each of us would dedicate ourselves 100 percent to our business. No "let's see," no "if I find time." Each person on the run would block everything else out for three months and focus solely on building their team, making contacts, holding presentations, growing personally, and staying laser focused.

When Sandro spoke about it, something clicked inside of me. I didn't just hear him—I understood him. And in that moment, I knew: this is my chance.

I made the decision to go all in—no compromises. That also meant setting clear boundaries. I told everyone—friends, acquaintances, even close loved ones:

"For the next ninety days, I'm fully focused on my business. Everything else will have to wait." It wasn't always easy. My husband and I love to go out and have a good time with our friends. But I knew exactly what I was doing and why I was doing it.

So I got to work. Not talking—doing.

Day after day, I had conversations, made calls, attended events, supported team members, kept learning, and broke through limits. It was intense. It was challenging.

And it was the best thing I've ever done.

When I started, I had a small team of about twenty people. After ninety days, we were 590 strong. And for the first time in my life, I held a five-figure paycheck in my hands.

That was the moment I didn't just realize that this works—I realized I work, when I decided to give it my all.

Those ninety days had been more than a business run. There had been a test, and I had passed. I felt transformed, like a new version of myself.

That new version of me knew my success wasn't luck. It was the result of a decision to run at full speed, giving relentless effort and an unshakable belief in the opportunity.

I learned many lessons on that run, but perhaps the most important was about the power that lies in a clear decision—how focus, discipline, and vision can completely change your life.

—Neuza

THE FUEL TO EXIT ORBIT

I found out about the 90-Day Run from one of Eric Worre's YouTube videos. I was so inspired, I immediately contacted the top members of my team.

"We have to do this!" I insisted.

They looked at me like I was crazy.

But once we'd been through the experience, no one was questioning that decision. In a matter of three months, our team went from 250 people to 4,200.

Ever since, I've been the biggest proponent of the 90-Day Run in network marketing. I've done seven in four years. As far as I know, I've now done more runs than any other major network marketer in the entire profession.

I love these runs because the 90-Day Run is **the most powerful strategy in network marketing**. Going on a run is like injecting rocket fuel into your network marketing rocket ship. It's no exaggeration that in three months, **you can take your business from a nice side income to a full-time thriving business**.

And this is really just the beginning of the benefits. A 90-Day Run also brings a team together, forging an identity as you all work as hard as you can together. As the head of the business, it proves your leadership to your recruits. *This is your chance to show your creative side, your inspiring side, and your motivating side.*

All that benefit in just ninety days.

WHAT IS A 90-DAY RUN?

So what is a 90-Day Run? In a way, this is nothing new. There are no more new techniques to learn. And if you've already taken over onboarding and presenting the business model from your sponsor, then there are no new responsibilities either.

Essentially, all you are going to do in a 90-Day Run is *put everything else in your life aside and work as hard as you can* in a very focused way to build your business. You'll be contacting more people, selling more product, and recruiting more people every day, every week, every month.

During this period, you *eliminate all possible distractions and add as much workload as you possibly can*. If you were working four hours a day on your business before, now you're working nine. If you were focused on the business three days a week before, you're now doing it all seven days of the week. The business becomes priority number one. Your other work, your family, your friends, your hobbies: everything else takes a backseat.

There's no hocus pocus, no special formula here. It's just complete focus on building your business. That's all it takes to achieve astounding success.

WHEN IS IT THE RIGHT TIME TO RUN?

Put in those terms, many new network marketers are ready to immediately jump into a 90-Day Run. Maybe that's the right choice for you, but first, you should really think through this decision. While the results are stupendous, *the effort required for a run is significant as well*. We call this a "run" because it's like training and running a marathon. It requires a lot of sacrifice, energy, focus, and motivation. And as the leader of your business, you need to always be out in front, showing others how it's done. You'll be the pace setter here. Where others might start grumbling and looking for an extra day off, you need to be up early, working every hour, bringing in more sales and recruits.

There's also certain issues you should consider ahead of time. First, *for a run to be truly effective, you need to already have achieved Core Rank*. It's technically possible to do a 90-Day Run before you get to that rank, but it's important to really know what you're doing to make the most of this process. It's an intense, time-consuming, energy-consuming period. So you want to make it count.

With that in mind, *you should also, ideally, already be comfortable doing onboarding and presentations*. Again, you can learn these things on the run, but you maximize results by having these skills already developed from the outset.

One of the reasons to reach Core Rank yourself before running is that I've seen people join a 90-Day Run and achieve Core Rank incredibly quickly because they have been influenced by the whole organization also running. *You want to be in a position to support those fast risers!*

Finally, *you need to be in a position to put everything else aside*. If you have a big vacation already booked for sometime over the next three months or your child's about to celebrate their first birthday, this might not be the time to go on a run.

All that said, you can really begin a 90-Day Run at any time. There's value in running immediately after your first month since you already have great momentum going. If you approach network marketing on this schedule, you could go from working full-time for someone else to running your business full-time in a total of four months.

It's also possible, though, to wait a month or two or six before you schedule your first run. There's no immediate rush if you aren't ready—but once you can commit, there should be no excuse to put it off.

PREPARING FOR THE RUN

Once you're committed, there's a significant amount of prep you need to do before you can even kick the run off. Like preparing for a marathon, you have to get your life in order to even commence with training.

With a 90-Day Run, you have to prepare your personal life, come up with a mission and goal, and figure out who is doing this run with you before you can even officially kickoff the preparation for the run!

PREPARE YOUR PERSONAL LIFE

What you're about to do is not ordinary. It goes way beyond what 95 percent of the people you know have ever done in their professional lives. It requires a huge amount of commitment on your part and on the part of everyone in your life.

To accomplish this, you need more than your own willingness and motivation. *You need everyone in your life aligned behind this run.*

So the first thing you need to do is ask everyone in your life if they are ready to support you through this. This is going to require your spouse to put the kids to sleep every night for ninety days. Your parents might not see you for those Sunday dinners for three months. Your friends are going to have to go out on Fridays without you. As much as possible, you also have to trim back work responsibilities.

To help get people on board, you can share the incredible upside to this run as well as the increased obligation and sacrifice. Ask if they are ready to support you for three months so all of you can benefit for the next nine months. Remind them that professional athletes regularly have to miss holidays or put off vacations because they have to commit to their careers above all else.

This is your moment. Can they help you achieve that dream?

And if they don't agree, that's okay. It's going to be harder for you, but you can still find the courage, belief, and energy to do this anyway!

FIND YOUR MISSION AND GOAL

Once your personal life is in order, you can turn your attention to the actual run. And the first step toward actually running is coming up with the mission and goal for your run. Like a marathon runner who sets a time they want to hit on the race, *you want to give your run a "theme" and set a concrete goal*.

For many, this is one of the more fun parts of network marketing. It's a creative exercise—a chance to come up with a fun idea that brings all this effort together and gives it purpose.

The mission and goal can really be *anything that speaks to you, your team, and the people you're trying to reach*. On my first run, I came up with the mission "Project 10K." Our goal was to sign up ten thousand new recruits by the end of the ninety days. The next run was called "Plan B: What If It Works." This run occurred just at the end of the pandemic, when people had recently lived through immense economic disruption. No one felt completely secure in their work anymore, so everyone needed a Plan B.

Everyone on the team was told to use this framing as an introduction to network marketing. This could be everyone's Plan B! It was a perfect conversation starter—a unique angle to bring in new people.

A year later, we did a sequel run called "Plan A: Because It Works." On that run, we told all the success stories that had come out of Plan B. We had so many people who had gone from making a few hundred euros a month to making thousands over the course of that year, all we had to do was tell those stories to anyone interested in network marketing.

Our most recent run was titled "Mission Possible: How to Turn Plans into Reality in Ninety Days." We leveraged all our experience doing 90-Day Runs to tell the story of the run itself to new recruits.

You might notice, the nature of the mission changed after that first run. Instead of focusing on the number of new recruits—a motivating concept within the team—every future run focused on motivating potential new recruits to the business. It was a theme that spoke to them, not to the people already involved.

You can develop a mission that motivates either your current team or those you hope join you, but you need that mission in place before you go any further. *This gives everyone clear instructions about what you're aiming to do and a sense of purpose behind the run.*

Ideally, you should aim to come up with this idea yourself. As the leader, you should put this mission together. If you're struggling, you can invite one or two others into the process, or else use AI or online suggestions to find a theme. Otherwise, you can end up with too many people trying to take ownership of the mission, which can lead to unnecessary friction.

FIND OUT WHO YOU'RE RUNNING WITH

With your mission in hand, it's time to find out who wants to join you on this run. It's important to say here that *you can absolutely do a 90-Day Run on your own*. You don't have to include your team at all. Now, the results compound the more people are involved, but if you want to really build your own network on a solo run, that can be a great option for some people.

Even if you do include your team, **you shouldn't expect everyone to sign up for this.** Life is busy. People have complex obligations and motivations. You may have found three months free of holidays, vacations, and work events, but others may have a busier schedule during that period. Or they just aren't willing to make the kind of sacrifices necessary for a run right now.

That's totally fine. When I did my first run, I asked for commitment upfront from people. Without even explaining what a run was, I asked who was with me on the next big adventure. Of the 250 people in my organization at the time, only sixty joined. But that sixty was with me through everything. Together, we brought in 4,200 new recruits over the next three months.

I don't recommend being as cryptic as I was with your team. Instead, share the potential of going on this run and the risk each person runs by missing out. I've seen many network marketers skip a run only to drop out of the profession entirely because they couldn't achieve the results they were looking for on their own.

Network marketing requires a delicate balance in communicating the urgency of these ideas without pushing people to do what they don't want to do. So, **after you explain the nature of the run, let each person make up their own mind if they're willing or able to commit right now.**

Now, the more people who do sign up, the better, obviously. When you have a team aligned around working ten hours a day instead of six, the results can be astounding. If you add those four hours a day to your own schedule, that's an extra twenty-eight hours of work on the business a week. That's great, but if you have nine others running with you, it's 280 extra hours. That's a lot of manpower!

That value decreases, however, if each of those nine is only half-motivated to run or if most of them drop out after a week or two. *What you want, then, is as many people as possible who are as motivated as you are by this process.*

START THE CLOCK

With your team locked in, it can be tempting to immediately start the race, but this is actually the moment when preparation truly begins. Unless you are doing a solo run—in which case, you can skip this section entirely—you need to give your team time to prepare for the work ahead.

So start the clock at thirty days. That's how long you should give everyone to get ready before the run commences.

That doesn't mean you are sitting on your hands all that time. Along with your normal network marketing work, *you should schedule a big kickoff call to formally announce the run*. This should be a big presentation where you announce the mission and the run's goal. You can pep everyone up and also let them know all they need to do to make the most of the run ahead.

As an additional bonus, you can invite prospects to the call as well. *The kickoff call can be an incredible recruitment tool.* Sell it to potential recruits as the best possible time to sign up: "You could start this journey at any time, but this is the best time because everyone is in hustler mode. Everyone is fully focused and committed right now. You'll never have more support or more potential to build your business than right now."

After the kickoff call, your responsibility is **making sure everyone else running is caught up on the major network marketing concepts they need to know**. Has everyone completed their onboarding? Do they all have their contact lists in place? Do they have some of the company's product that they regularly use? Have they set their own long-term business goal?

Remember, each person on this run needs just as much preparation as you do, organizing their lives and getting support at home. The aim here is to avoid anyone getting an "injury" from this run. So provide as much support as each person needs. It benefits everyone if all the runners are in optimal condition to go all out for the full ninety days.

COUNTDOWN CHECKLIST

3. Commit to your first 90-Day Run at a time when you can scale back all personal and professional commitments.

2. Create a mission and goal to give your run a theme.

1. Find out which recruits want to run with you, then give the whole team thirty days to prepare.

CHAPTER 9

THE NONSTOP SPRINT

Imagine it:

You're twenty-six days in, and you haven't taken a break. You're so tired that you're struggling to get out of bed in the morning. At breakfast, you're still a zombie. You've noticed you're drinking an extra pot of coffee some days just to get through your whole list of tasks. You begin to question yourself every time you look in the mirror.

Is this sustainable?

But you know the answer. No matter how tired you are, you're locked in. You know that this is the only way to get from today to the future you've been dreaming of. Before this journey, you never thought you'd achieve that dream. It was something you kept tucked away in your heart. You never expected it to see the light of day. How could you give up now?

So you begin Day 26. You open your computer and begin taking on task after task. You call potential customers. You reach out to five people you met last week who were interested in joining you on this journey but were still on the fence. Do they have any questions? Can you explain any concepts in more detail?

Then you take a deep breath, pour another cup of coffee, and log into the team meeting. From somewhere deep inside, you find the enthusiasm to motivate the team. You review progress, make sure everyone else is still checking off their tasks, and push everyone to work as hard as they possibly can for the next hour. It's an all-out sprint—no excuses, even if it's at the end of the day.

You log out, exhausted.

But then, you see a message from your sponsor or upline.

"How did you recruit this many people this quickly? These numbers are incredible!"

Attached, you see how much you've earned so far this month—but that can't be right. Is that triple what you made the month before?

Suddenly, you feel energized for the first time in weeks. Not only can you do this—you are doing it. If this is your business after twenty-six days, what is it going to look like after ninety?

Forget about rest. Forget about sleep. Why not work on a few more social media posts? Why not email a couple more people about the company catalogue you sent them last week? Why not keep going?

You've got this. You're just getting started.

—You

UNLOCK YOUR OBSESSION

For your run to really pay off, you have to bring energy every single day over three solid months. The magic of a 90-Day Run only really happens when you take all your knowledge, experience, and motivation from your career in network marketing so far and turn the intensity up to one hundred.

The word I like to use here is **obsession**. During a run, I'm often so locked in that I forget to eat. I forget to go to bed. When I do remember to get some sleep, I lie awake, staring at the ceiling, thinking about the next big task ahead. I'm so excited to write that next post or reach out to that new contact, sometimes, I just get up again and get back to work.

When you're truly obsessed, the 90-Day Run is like living in an unending flow state. *It's ninety days doing everything, all the time, all at once.* You're posting on all of your social media accounts, making new connections everywhere you go, reaching out to old customers, doing onboarding and presentations and sales, all in one day.

Of course, you don't have to take your obsession quite as far as I do. Remember, you're your own boss now. You determine how hard you're going to work and how seriously you're going to take this run. No one is going to be standing behind you, looking over your shoulder, and pushing you to stay up a little longer or make one more call. If you want to turn this run into more of a jog, that's your choice.

But the harder you go on this run, the better the results. *If you want to change your life in a single season, you need to be obsessed with that project.*

STAY ON TASK

Passion is so powerful during a run, but it isn't everything. The reason I focused so much on prep in the last chapter is that it's so easy to get sidetracked. Sometimes, it can feel like everything is conspiring to keep you from putting everything into this run. The kids will keep you up all night. Friends will call and ask for favors or ask if you want to hang out. Your parents will say they really miss you and wish you could come visit again. No matter how hard you've tried to free up your schedule, things will come up. And you'll need more than dedication to your run to avoid distraction.

The best way to make sure you're running at full speed is to block time on your calendar. Those blocked-off periods should be 100 percent dedicated to network marketing activities—and IPAs (income producing activities) in particular.

If you just try to squeeze in network marketing during your run, those IPAs will be the first thing you abandon as other responsibilities come up. If you've ever tried to get in shape without carving out a set time to work out each day, you know how this goes. The first week, you might manage to find time to hit the weights every day. But by Week 2, things start to pile up. There's that TV show you promised to watch with your spouse and that project at work that you need to come in early to finish. So you miss a day or two. Each time, you tell yourself you're just going to skip this one session, but by Week 4, you're missing the gym most days. Within another month, you give up entirely.

So block that time off and make it nonnegotiable. Once you have a set schedule, fill it with concrete activities. *Give yourself a daily to-do list* that includes everything you have to achieve in a day. It might look something like:

- Add three more contacts to your list of names.
- Identify ten new contacts to connect with on social media.
- Like some pictures, comment on a few posts, and find something in common with these new contacts.
- Follow up with five customers who have bought products from you in the past.
- Follow up with five prospects who have had some sort of exposure to your company and considered potentially joining your team.
- Send your company's catalogue to ten new prospective customers.

You can adjust these tasks as necessary to meet the needs of your company. And keep in mind that it's always okay during a run to go above and beyond these requirements. ***This list should represent the bare minimum you'll accomplish each day during those times you've blocked off.***

HELP YOUR TEAM SUCCEED

If you're running with a team, part of your job is making it as likely as possible that each runner succeeds. Organization and motivation are just as important for your team members as they are for you. If anything, your recruits are more likely than you to push off these responsibilities an hour, a day, or a week at a time. Before they know it, they'll have missed the whole run. Your job is to do everything in your power to make sure that doesn't happen.

One reason your team needs this support is that **runs can also be a time when people lose faith in network marketing if they aren't careful.** One tricky element of network marketing is that there's an inescapable, short delay between putting in the effort and seeing results. **It takes a few weeks of running for the concrete rewards to start coming in.** That's how long it takes for people to buy products, go to a presentation, decide to join, and start on their own journey—and it's how long it takes for your company to start rewarding you for those behaviors.

Three weeks is a long time to put in this much effort, especially if your motivation is wavering. That's where your people are going to need you. You need to be there to help keep your team members focused on those rewards—you're the one who can help inspire them to make it over that last hill.

Your team may also need your help organizing their time. For that reason, you should share to-do lists with everyone.

You can bring these two responsibilities—motivation and organization—together with a special kind of meeting called a "blitz hour." These are weekly, one-hour meetings in which everyone meets up in a CoWork or on a shared Zoom call and then follows your concrete instructions on how to use that hour to their maximal benefit. The whole hour, everyone works side-by-side, checking off activities and making real progress building their business.

The blitz hour is only one of the meetings you should be holding every week. **You should also increase the number of presentations you do, from one to two each week.** That way, no prospect ever has to wait more than three days to go to a presentation.

They're far more likely to feel the urgency and momentum of the moment if they can get to a presentation sooner and see how locked in everyone is.

CATCHING YOUR BREATH

The 90-Day Run is at once an unending sprint and a long marathon. If that sounds exhausting, it is. It's normal that you and members of your team need some kind of break. At the same time, you have to maintain momentum, motivation, and focus for this exhausting effort to be worth it.

The compromise I've developed is called *"30-1, 30-1, 30-none."* You work nonstop for thirty days, then you take one off. Then you work another thirty days and take one more day off. If you do that one more time, you're at the end of the run!

On that special day off, make sure to use it to your full advantage. If you have kids, spend the whole day with them and let them choose the activity for that day. If it's just your spouse, they can set the schedule. Otherwise, spend it with friends or recharge in any way that works best for you.

Everyone on the team should take this day at the end of each month. It's helpful to know there's a moment to catch your breath before racing off again.

Of course, some people will want more rest than that. Like a trainer helping someone prepare for a marathon, you have to be supportive, empathetic, and motivating when someone says they just can't go any farther. Just like when recruiting people for the run, ***you have to strike the balance of communicating*** *the urgency of the moment without forcing anyone to do what they don't want to do.*

Tell your team member that you know how hard this is, but remind them that this is the start of a new life. If they really feel they need a break, tell them that's okay. They can take a minute, an hour, or a day to catch their breath. Of course, every break means a little less progress on their business. The more they do, the better the results. The easier they take it, the slower they'll rise.

If you have some people lagging far behind the rest of the group, it's important to remain understanding. After all, they aren't your employees. They're on their own network marketing journeys with their own businesses. *At the same time, though, you should put most of your effort into those who prove they share your obsession.*

The 90-Day Run is a long, hard road. Focus on running it with those who truly believe in putting in the effort for the incredible potential at the finish line.

IMAGINE THE END

One day off a month is not much. A run is grueling, and it's natural to start getting exhausted. And it's natural to start slowing down at some point.

When I see someone slowing down on a run, I recommend a particular exercise. I tell them to *close their eyes and imagine they're at the next big company convention*. The run is over and in the past. At the convention, they get to enjoy the fruits of all that effort. I tell them to **imagine the rank they've achieved** because they kept pushing themselves during the run.

They imagine their entire team is there, going crazy to celebrate this achievement. Their family is present, tearing up because **they're so proud.**

They sit in that vision, imagining how they'll feel in that moment, living that future life. **Isn't that future worth running toward**, even if you're tired?

It's a powerful way to reenergize yourself and find that extra bit of motivation when times are tough.

COUNTDOWN CHECKLIST

3. Block off time each day for your network marketing activities and create a to-do list to make sure you always make concrete progress.

2. Share your to-do list and remember to keep motivating your team during the run.

1. Take one day off at the end of each month to recharge, then get back to running! If you're still struggling, imagine a moment in the near future when the run is over and you're enjoying all the success from your effort.

CHAPTER 10

CONSOLIDATE YOUR SUCCESS

I woke up the morning after my first run in a completely new world. Before I started, my team had roughly 250 members. Now, it was nearly twenty times that size, at about 4,200.

This was an incredible success—so much so, I couldn't even feel disappointed that I'd fallen short of the ten thousand new recruits I'd set ninety-one days before.

Still, I'm not the sort to pat myself on the back too much. Instead, I got back to work. I knew that the only way to build on my run was to actually consolidate those new recruits into a new team. Obviously, I couldn't do that alone. There is no way one person can reach out to four thousand people and make sure they are all progressing along their path to network marketing success.

Instead, I organized that outreach through all the team members who had reached Core Rank or above. Each to connect with the new members in their downline.

I wasn't done yet. Next, I set up new "business as usual" standards, helping all 4,200 of us go from 200 percent back to 100 percent. This is essential after any burst of growth in business. It's very tricky for people to go from racing at full speed back down to a pace they can maintain every day. And it's a particularly dangerous period for those new to network marketing. I knew that some people would still be struggling to shake their "employee mentality." They weren't ready yet to fully embrace the responsibility that comes with all that entrepreneurial freedom. So I developed tasks that everyone should complete each day, allowing the "employee" types to keep advancing while they shook off that mindset.

Then I got to the fun stuff. When I teach network marketers about leadership, I always introduce one tool in particular: The Top 50 List. Every successful network marketer should have a list of fifty people spread across their whole organization who are the best performing, most influential, and most ambitious. These are the people you can rely on to keep building the company if you decide you want to take a year off to travel the world, learn how to paint sunsets, or whatever.

Importantly, you don't choose these leaders based on emotions. You choose them based on performance. And there's no better time to judge performance than a 90-Day Run.

A run is basically designed to test your limits. You see what you're really made of—and what everyone else is made of too. By the end, you know who has what it takes.

But you can't just eyeball that.

So during those ninety days, I monitored the performance of every member of the team. I kept track of personal sales, personal recruits, rank advancement, and so on.

By the end, I had a fully fleshed out Top 50. I knew who the leaders were in the organization and who had the most future potential.

All of that was a lot of work coming right after a three-month sprint, but I discovered that I wasn't exhausted by that run. I was energized. I was more committed and ready to go than ever before.

—SANDRO

TAKE A BREAK

The day after your run ends, you may wake up to find your whole life has changed. You'll now have a substantial organization behind you. From making $500 a month when you achieved Core Rank, you may be making thousands upon thousands of dollars a month now. I've seen people come out of this process more than doubling their income—when they were already making a good living.

There's still a lot to do, but before you jump up and start running again, *give yourself a chance to rest.* For ninety days, you've been going almost nonstop. *You've never deserved a reward more in your life.* So take a little time off for yourself. If you can, I recommend taking a vacation somewhere sunny and relaxing.

And don't just reward yourself. After all, everyone in your life made sacrifices to make this possible. Your kids, your spouse, your parents, your friends, maybe even your boss at your full-time job: they've all done their part to make this run possible.

Take the time to reconnect with people and show your gratitude. Go out with friends on Friday and pay for everyone's dinner. Take your parents to a ball game and get them great seats. And just hang out and play with your kids. This is a chance to reestablish normal life and recharge your battery. Enjoy it. You've earned it.

TAKE STOCK

Once you're back to work, it's time to take stock of the run. How did it go? In business, there's a common expression, **"A successful project should include three steps: plan, do, review."** To review, you can start by looking at the numbers. How many people did you have in your organization before? How many do you have now? How much product were you selling before the run, and how much are you selling today?

But this isn't the only way to review the run. You should **consider your personal experience of the run**. What parts did you find hardest? How did you maintain your motivation? You can then **ask people in your organization** to see where you got things right and where you made mistakes.

Put another way, if you don't review, you haven't really finished your 90-Day Run. The review is almost as important as the run itself. You may learn things that change how you run your business or prepare for your next run. For instance, when reviewing our second run, I discovered that many people felt we had too many meetings. People felt that they didn't have time to focus on IPAs because we were always on calls instead of reaching out to new potential customers and recruits. On the next run, I made some critical adjustments. I added more blitz hours with focus on IPAs. Then I delegated those blitz hours to team leaders so that the meetings were smaller and everyone could work more closely together. The results improved immensely!

Some of the lessons you learn from your run you can implement immediately. Perhaps your team felt you needed to answer your phone more often, a change you can commit to as soon as you get the feedback. Other info may have to be earmarked for the next run. *But any information that improves your organization is valuable, so seek it out.* Don't just go back to business as usual.

ENROLLING ALL YOUR NEW RECRUITS

There's one more crucial step you must take before getting back to business as usual: *making sure every new team member is fully integrated and plugged into the organization.* You've just brought in a huge number of new recruits over three months. It's easy for some people to slip through the cracks.

Over the course of your first week back after your break, you should reach out to everyone on your team who ran with you and *make sure all their new recruits (and the new recruits of those recruits) are receiving the support and resources they need to become successful network marketers in their own right.*

Everyone should be getting a proper onboarding. Everyone should be getting the necessary materials. All new recruits should have a sponsor who is actively engaged in their progress—answering their questions, motivating them to continue building their business, and handling onboarding and presentations for the recruit's new recruits.

Just because you have ten times the head count to keep track of, that's no excuse for letting someone miss out on the incredible opportunity network marketing represents. Remember, that's someone's dream that might not be fulfilled. It's someone's chance to live their life on their terms that might not be realized. Everyone deserves the best possible chance to succeed in this profession.

So take the time to consolidate the team, and as early as possible, reach out and meet all the new recruits. Provide support where you're needed while helping your more experienced team members to fly on their own.

Of course, even if you are completely engaged in this consolidation, some new recruits are naturally going to drift away. These are people who got swept up in the excitement of the run, who may have agreed to join on impulse, but who never really committed.

It's totally okay and expected that these recruits will drop out of your network sooner or later (usually sooner). While you should reach out to these people and give them a chance, you should accept their decision at the moment. You can always contact them again later to see if they're ready to come back and join you.

PASSING ON THE SYSTEM

The guidelines I've shared in this book up to this point are a **system**. Systems need to be understood and applied. That's what we've been working on so far. But they require one other component, as well: *they must be passed on to the next generation.*

This is called duplication, and after your first run (or shortly after achieving Core Rank if you put your run off for a while), that becomes *one of your chief jobs*. It will be up to you to make sure everybody in your organization understands, applies, and duplicates the system.

This is the crucial next step if you want to build a long-term sustainable business that will bring you to the moon.

This is actually what it means to build a business, build a company, and become an entrepreneur. Your path to freedom requires systems!

THIS ISN'T YOUR LAST RUN

After your first run, your network marketing rocket ship will most likely be ready to shoot off and burst out of the atmosphere, with the moon growing ever closer. This is an incredible, life-changing experience. It's easy to get so wrapped up in it that you forget that *this isn't the end of the journey*.

Indeed, while it's fine to stop thinking about running for a bit, you should always keep in mind that *you will need to repeat this process—and the sooner the better*.

This is where I break with many of the profession's leading thinkers. Some network marketing experts recommend doing one or two runs in a career. *I think you should do them once a year.* Now, that may feel unsustainable to you at this point, but the fact remains, the more you run, the bigger and more resilient your organization will become. If you really want to get to the moon—and beyond—you'll need to build 90-Day Runs regularly into your schedule.

We're talking about the potential to secure generational wealth for your family here. If that's what you're in this business for, you need to run regularly.

In fact, when you come to see runs as a regular business strategy, you can find additional uses for them in your business. A run isn't just there to provide a one-time boost to your business. It can also help you shake things up. In times when you and your team are losing motivation or results are lagging, *a run can shake off the stagnation*.

Nothing brings a team together and builds mutual success like a run. They're tough, exhausting events, but like a marathon, they really whip your organization into shape.

NEXT STOP: THE MOON

Once you've finished your run and consolidated your success, all that's left for you to do is to keep moving in the same direction as the moon gets ever closer. The only thing that can throw you off now is taking your hands off the steering wheel and assuming the work is done.

There's still work to do. Most importantly, now is the time to solidify everything you've built: adding the structure to make this more than a one-time success.

COUNTDOWN CHECKLIST

3. Once your run is over, take a well-deserved vacation to recharge.

2. Review the run from every angle: look at the numbers of new recruits and products sold, your personal impression of the run, and the feedback from your team.

1. Consolidate your success by making sure every new recruit is receiving all the materials and support they need to build their own network marketing business.

PART IV

APPROACHING THE MOON

CHAPTER 11

THE MOON
LANDING

It was December 7, 2020—a date that has been engraved in my heart. I was sitting with Sandro. In just a few minutes, he explained this business to me. No long speeches, no endless slides. Just words that made something inside me resonate.

In particular, Sandro said that one sentence that has stayed with me ever since: "Edita, this is the train that only passes once in a lifetime."

In that very moment something unexplainable happened: I saw a picture in my mind. A vision. A door was opening, and behind it, I saw a life bigger, freer, and more fulfilling than anything I had ever imagined.

Within fifteen minutes, my decision was made.

"This is exactly the one I've been waiting for," I told him.

The following three months were a battle between heart and duty. By day, I continued my responsible life as an employee. By night, my heart beat for that vision of freedom and growth that would not let me go. I had sleepless nights as I waged an inner battle, caught between two worlds.

During that time, Sandro was more than just a business partner. He was my anchor. He knew the pressure I felt, the fear of letting someone down. He listened and understood and found a way to keep me motivated. His firmness and his unshakable belief in our shared vision only strengthened my own.

On March 30th, 2021, I made the decision: All in. No more halfway measures. On April 1st, my new life began—free, self-determined, and filled with a burning passion. From that moment on, everything entered a new dimension. The vision grew, the results came, and I kept pushing beyond what I had always assumed were my limits.

These years have shaped me more than decades of working as an employee. I didn't just find a business—I found my calling.

I became an entrepreneur.

Today I know: December 7, 2020, was my second birthday.

—Edita

* * *

I had been there from the beginning, as a co-founder of our network marketing organization, contributing to the shape of our community. I built structures, codeveloped the community, and trained people. I was selling and recruiting, building a business and a team, and watching as everything took off.

But for a long time, I couldn't fully enjoy the potential of this profound opportunity because I couldn't fully let go of my former life. I had a good job as a project manager at a leading banking software company, and I was struggling to leave that security behind. I had a good salary, bonuses, and benefits. I got to work from home. It wasn't the career I wanted, but it was hard to convince myself to throw it away.

Still, my heart was telling me the job wasn't right for me. My heart was with the network company I was building.

Network marketing could offer me something that my job couldn't. It gave me freedom, purpose, and the chance to create something of my own. That's what I wanted in my life, but month after month, I felt the income wasn't enough to justify quitting.

Month after month, I felt like I was living a double life. During the work week, I was a project manager. Then, with every moment of my free time, I was a network marketer. I attended events, joined Practice Days on weekends, and even traveled abroad for training and meetings. Sandro, with his unshakable belief and vision, always gave me the support I needed to keep pushing forward, even when it was exhausting.

About a year into my network marketing journey, I knew I had to make a call. I'd seen that Sandro's leadership and the process he was developing really worked. But I was never going to be able to get where I wanted to go in my business if I kept one foot in my old life. I had to go all in if I wanted to achieve extraordinary results.

So I finally did it. I quit my job. No more safety net, no more Plan B. I was going to put everything in network marketing.

The result was almost instantaneous. I went up two ranks in my organization and saw my revenue multiply in a very short time. Before I knew it, I had the income I had been chasing for a year and was able to continue to dedicate myself to my business while enjoying the lifestyle I wanted.

It was only possible because I finally decided to put 100 percent focus into achieving my dream.

—Alessandro

TIME FOR FULL TIME

Once you've caught your breath after your first 90-Day Run and brought your new team together, you are likely to face a huge decision for the first time: **are you ready to go all in**? Some of you may have already made this decision. Perhaps you went full-time as soon as you started, or maybe you made the leap at the beginning of your run. For most, though, this represents yet another moment to recommit. This is when you decide to leave the escape pod behind and go full throttle toward the moon.

Of course, exactly when this moment appears is different for each of us. It may still be months away for you. Or it may be today. But after that first run, you should definitely be able to see it over the horizon.

To determine when it's right to fully commit, **you can trust your gut or rely on your sponsor's advice**. But sometimes, sponsors are helpful, and it's always nice to have a more concrete reason for a big change. When you think the time is approaching, return to that long-term goal you set way back at the beginning of your time in network marketing. That goal listed where you wanted to land on the moon.

So, how close are you now? If you wanted to make $5,000 a month, you may already be deploying the landing gear. In that case, why not quit and go all in on growing your business from there? However, if you were looking to make $15,000 to not just replace but double your current income—and your network marketing business is only making $5,000 a month at the moment—perhaps it's better to hold off a bit longer.

There's no right answer here because network marketing is all about you setting your own goals and deciding when you hit them. There are 120 million network marketers out there, but only 10 percent do it full-time. And only 3 percent feel they are truly successful. The reason for that low number is at least in part because we all define success differently—and **many don't set a concrete measure to know when they've truly made it**.

Only you can decide if you're ready to land, if you're close enough to take a leap of faith, or if you need a bit more time. This is your business, your journey, and your life. You make the call. Just know, sooner or later, you'll have to make it if you want to keep growing.

BUILDING YOUR MOON BASE

Whether you're ready to go full-time into network marketing or not, your moon landing site should be coming into view. Depending on your ultimate goals in network marketing you may be preparing to land or still have some distance to go, but you should be getting ever closer to the moon.

As you prepare for your first moonwalk, it's time for one more reminder of the mindset required once you're there. You've succeeded, and you deserve immense credit for that, but this isn't a get-rich-quick kind of business. Instead, **the moon is really just the beginning**. Once you're there, you're now among the elite crowd of successful entrepreneurs working around the world. And **like all great entrepreneurs, you have to keep building**.

This may seem obvious, but it's easy to forget when you get up there. Down here on Earth, looking up at the night sky, I'm sure you're confident you'd keep working after you get that first big paycheck. But one of the most difficult things to do for someone who has never been self-employed or been this successful is continuing to remain motivated once you achieve success. The onboarding is done. The run is complete. You now have more money coming into your account than ever before. It's tempting to feel like you've won the lottery and just sit back and enjoy your reward for the hard work you've already done.

This perspective can lead to a very short trip to the moon. Half of the work your team will do is based on the inspiration they take from your example. You have to demonstrate the work ethic, responsibility, and investment in your business that you want to see in others. **If you start taking it easy, you can expect everyone you've recruited to start doing the same.** In that case, don't be surprised if you check in on your business some day and find half your team has left and half your income has disappeared. **Once your rocket starts losing altitude, it can be hard to reverse course.**

Put another way, **you will either be the engine or the brake for your team**. Either you push everyone forward or you hold them all back. If you want to continue to be a success in network marketing, you can't just sit back and manage what you have, you have to keep building—and helping others do the same.

To help wrap your mind around this, imagine your business is actually a physical store. If your store became a huge success, and you started making your dream income from it, would you decide to stop showing up, hand the keys to one of your employees, and expect your customers and team to keep things running like normal?

Of course not. That's likely to lead to a sudden drop in sales, with employees failing to show up for work and customers looking for other options. The same principle applies to your network marketing business. *If you aren't putting the work in every day, it's going to fall apart even more quickly than you built it.* Just when you thought you were about to reach the moon, you might be in for a crash landing.

STRENGTHEN YOUR SYSTEMS

Of course, work is going to start looking a little different once you're on the moon. You'll be running a mature business, and that comes with a different set of responsibilities. While you'll still need to do the basic network marketing tasks of selling and recruiting, it's important to also attend to all these business considerations.

YOU'RE THE EXPERT

The first thing you'll have to do is embrace your role as an expert in every part of the network marketing system. *Remember how you looked at your sponsor and the rest of your upline when you first began? That is now how your downline looks at you.* You have to be the master of onboarding and presentations. You're the one they expect to have a clear answer on all the big questions.

As the expert, you may have to start developing new materials to help your downline. Whether it's new sales materials for new products or improved explanations for onboarding, you should know better than anyone what information is missing and how to supply it.

BUILD YOUR CORE TEAM AND COMMUNICATION SYSTEM

That's a lot of responsibility, but luckily, you aren't alone in this business. Once you're on the moon, you'll want to select those members of your team you can really rely on. These seven or so people should represent your core moon crew. They are the ones you'll continue to build the organization through.

Once you have your crew in mind, it's time to improve your communication systems. **You need to make sure each person in the organization gets the information they need to succeed— not too much or too little.** In my business, we use WhatsApp because it's easy to set up different chats for people at different rankings so we can adjust communication at each level. There's a saying I love: "You don't feed a burger to a newborn." In our context, it means that **you don't want someone new to the organization to deal with all the complexities of someone closer to the top**. At the same time, you can't expect your moon crew to succeed if you're trying to feed them formula instead of that burger. This kind of hierarchy of information is well-known to established businesses. Now that your business is established, you'll need a similar hierarchy of your own.

Keep in mind, though, that just because you now have seven team members you work particularly closely with, that doesn't mean you can ignore everyone else. **You should continue to connect with everyone who joins your organization.** After all, future lunar leaders could come from anywhere in the organization. **The next great network marketer may have just joined your team last week!** You need to be on top of this situation and aware of who has real potential, as well as who needs (and deserves) some extra support.

Importantly, you also have to establish a certain level of professionalism within your organization. Whether it's your core team or a new recruit, you should be friendly but avoid making this whole enterprise about friendship. This can be a difficult balance to maintain because you may have entered into network marketing with friends and because of friends.

To maintain success, though, you need to create a certain amount of distance. You have to provide support and a positive atmosphere while avoiding making things too personal.

This may feel like a lot of work—and it is—but once again, imagine your business is a store. You wouldn't run a store without meeting the new person running the cash register or stocking your shelves, right? You need to know they've been fully trained, and, hey, they may end up becoming a future manager.

And you wouldn't run your store like a place to just get together and hang out either. You'd want everyone to have a good time—but you'd have to keep your eye focused on the business first.

A good store owner meets every new member of the team, gets to know them a bit, and finds out if they need any additional guidance. They also set the tone and show what professionalism looks like. This is your store, so own that role.

MASTER YOUR SCHEDULE

After finishing your first run, creating a long-term work schedule shouldn't be too difficult for you. After all, you already blocked off time for the run. ***Once you're back to "business as usual," you can scale that back slightly to make it manageable on a week-by-week basis.***

But that's not the only scheduling you'll need to do. ***You also need to determine a cadence of meetings for your whole organization***, including a weekly "stand-up" meeting, presentations, and more.

In my business, we have our stand-up meeting every Monday morning. These are very popular in tech, which is where I started my career. Essentially, ***you gather all your moon crew together, share any important news, mention priorities and goals for the week, and give them a boost of motivation***. These meetings also communicate expectations to everyone in your network. If you don't expect people to show up, they won't show up. If you don't give them goals, they won't achieve them.

You also need to set a time for your weekly company presentation and two coaching sessions with your team—one about products and one about network marketing techniques and strategies.

With those weekly meetings permanently set on the calendar, *you need to start planning the next run.* As I've already mentioned, you should ideally do a run every year. *Each annual run should include your moon crew and the growing number of people who volunteer to join you.*

Regular runs are so important because **network marketing growth tends to come in waves.** There's a big rush of new recruits or new sales and then a quiet period afterward. Runs allow you to take control of this process, creating the wave yourself.

Once you are working full-time on your business, I recommend *planning your annual run for the first half of the year.* The reason for this is that the last quarter of the year is almost always the period of strongest growth. It's the holiday season and a time when people look at their lives and want to try something new. So, if you recruit new team members in the first half of the year, they'll be fully onboarded and selling and recruiting in time for that last quarter, which will give each of them a chance to jump up the ranks in their first year.

PLANNING YOUR FIRST EVENT

Relatedly, now is the time to step into event planning. **Network marketing is famous for its event culture. It's one of our profession's superpowers.** These events offer everyone a chance to get together, socialize, motivate one another, have fun, and learn a lot. So you don't want to leave these out of your growing organization.

There are different types of events you should begin planning, each on a different schedule. First, **you should offer a monthly educational meeting.** This is a more in-depth meeting than the weekly training you already provide.

Twice a year, you should offer a similar meeting focused solely on developing your moon crew. Once again, this meeting is primarily educational. In both cases, you'll want to make this a fun and enjoyable gathering of colleagues, but priority has to be placed on everyone getting better acquainted with some of the more advanced tools of network marketing.

From there, you get to focus on the really fun stuff. **Once a year, you should throw a big party for your whole organization.** I call this the "moon run" event in my business. It's a chance for everyone to get together and just celebrate our success.

The last event isn't really one you have to plan, but you should plan to attend it. This is the event thrown by your partner company. They'll introduce new products, share some educational information, and then let everyone have a good time together.

At each of your events, **you should schedule time to recognize the achievements of your team.** By the time you have your second moon crew event or your first big annual party, you may have forgotten how incredible it felt to achieve Core Rank, but it's a big deal to the person who just joined your organization a couple months ago. **Network marketing is all about building one another up and supporting each other so we all succeed.** This isn't like a traditional business where you have to wait for your boss to tap you on the shoulder once a year before mumbling well done; in this profession, we make a point of recognizing success regularly at these events. We see you're working hard, we see your success, and we celebrate you.

In some ways, that's the most powerful motivator of all.

TIME TO GET ON SOCIAL MEDIA

Finally, now is the time to embrace social media if you haven't already. I recommend you go back and read my thoughts on this from earlier in the book. To recap, briefly, social media should be a place where you build an identity that speaks to your authentic interests. ***Don't turn your Instagram account into a nonstop blitz of ads and discounts for your network marketing products.***

To really get a handle on how to build this identity, I recommend following the master of this topic, Frazer Brookes, and reading his bestseller *I Dare You*. When I joined his group to learn about social media, he was remarkably insightful. In particular, he taught me that the best way to sell products from my network marketing company (which focuses on perfumes) was to use social media to talk about what I really loved most.

Since I love offering business advice, that became central to my online identity. And I've grown an enormous following from it.

I do post on social media about my travels and my organization. I sometimes post about the nice pens I've acquired. And I share advice for upcoming entrepreneurs in network marketing and elsewhere. ***That's all authentic to me, and crucially, it feels authentic to my followers.***

I've seen incredibly successful network marketers clean up

online just by becoming popular members of a Facebook group about their favorite dog breed or their love of growing house plants. Once people come to know you and like you for that interest, they're far more open to giving your products a try or taking a chance on network marketing.

THE MOON…AND BEYOND

If you do all this right, you can end up in a virtuous cycle of constant growth: a world of unlimited success that can allow you to go beyond the moon and explore the galaxy of your wildest dreams.

But before I wish you bon voyage, there's one more message I have to share with you: don't forget to bring everyone else along. Because network marketing doesn't just have the power to change your life; it could change the way we do business forever.

COUNTDOWN CHECKLIST

3. Decide if now is the time to go full-time and all in on your network marketing business.

2. Maintain motivation even after you hit your initial business goals.

1. Invest time into building the systems that will allow your business to keep growing.

CHAPTER 12

A CHANCE TO EXPLORE THE STARS

It was our big annual event. Eighteen hundred people had flown in from all across Europe and beyond. Standing on stage in front of all of them, I had the opportunity to make a long-held dream of mine come true. I invited my father on stage. At sixty-two, he'd worked hard to provide for my family his whole adult life. He'd been an example to me for as long as I've been alive. On that stage, I was able to give him a gift he richly deserved. I told him, "You've done enough. You don't have to work another day for the rest of your life."

Normally, I wouldn't do this sort of thing publicly. I'm a naturally introverted person, and I like to keep my private life to myself. But I felt I had to share this moment with everyone there because each of them had contributed to this moment, and each of them were on a path to achieve those same possibilities.

The people who have followed me on this journey now run successful businesses of their own—some even have real employees who run their social media or handle their IT needs. Every day, they are achieving their dreams and helping others get to that same place in their lives.

Standing there with my father, looking out at that audience—our whole team gathered in celebration of this moment—I had one final dream in mind: I want to share this possibility with as many people as possible.

—SANDRO

IN THE YEAR 2050…

I have a vision of the future. It's not a future of flying cars or teleportation (although those would be cool). It's a future of constant lunar travel for everyone brave enough to take a chance on building their own rocket to the moon.

In that future, network marketing is no longer looked at with suspicion. It no longer has to deal with scams because the real businesses have won the day. They've proven the economic value of this business model to the world.

Because the world of business has been won over, there's been a transition from traditional stores and e-commerce to an ethical, social business model that shares wealth and changes lives.

From 120 million mostly part-time network marketers, this future world hosts more than a billion, with a large percentage making their business their main source of income. The most successful companies use this model to share their products with the world. The most successful network marketing leaders have their names and photos in *Forbes* next to the other major entrepreneurs and CEOs. As more and more people become network marketing professionals, the profession brings in trillions in sales each year.

Everyone on the planet has a readily available opportunity to join a high-quality network marketing organization, work for themselves, and take their own trip to the moon.

That's my dream. And it was a huge motivation behind writing this book. I want to help you build a network marketing rocket ship that will take you to the moon, but to achieve this dream, I need you to keep going once you're there. To share the incredible power of network marketing, I need people with big dreams like you to help the rest of the world build their own rockets and shoot for the stars.

If we work at this together, we'll make this future a reality far sooner than 2050.

PROFESSIONALIZE THE PROFESSION

The first way you can contribute to this vision is by **being a role model for the profession**. So many people still assume all network marketing operations are scams. I've tried to be forthright and honest about the scams that have and still do exist in this profession, but the best way to convince the world of the positive potential in network marketing is for people like you to show that potential to others.

It won't just be the people you've already recruited who look at you as an example. Others who remain skeptical will also be watching. Those friends on your initial 150-person contact list who said no will stand to the side and wait to see if you get scammed or start scamming other people. *If, instead, you turn into a successful, driven businessperson, you may just win over those cynics.*

At the same time, when you're motivating your people or speaking about the value of this profession, don't get stuck describing the material wealth you can or have achieved. Look, I've done very well in network marketing. I have some very nice cars and very nice watches. I have several very nice, expensive pens, and I wear nice suits. I get to travel to some very luxurious locations for work and for vacation. But you may have noticed that I didn't brag about any of those things in this book. That's been intentional. *Wealth is a wonderful thing to possess, but the real value of network marketing isn't that it can make some people wealthy; it's that it can allow people to work for themselves and achieve their dreams.* They can do work they believe in, work the way they want to, and feel fulfilled in their work.

That's the vision I want to sell to the world. And I hope you'll help me do so.

HELPING OTHERS CLIMB

Of course, the most direct way you can help me achieve this vision is by simply growing your business. The more people you turn into network marketing successes, the bigger and better your business—and the closer we all are to elevating network marketing to the position it should hold in modern business.

But there are two ways you can recruit and grow your business. You can convince as many people as possible to sign up using whatever promises you can think of, get them to work in this profession for six months, make a little money, and then mostly disengage. Or **you can help them build a business that reaches as high as their ambitions will take them**.

The second option is better business for you, better for them, and better for network marketing.

I hope the second option is the one you favor. Help those who have dreams as grand as yours. Their rise will help you rise. Everyone wins, and we'll have one more advocate for network marketing.

A FLEET ROCKETS EXPLORING THE GALAXY

This book will help you get to the moon and enjoy your dreams. But for network marketing to change the world the way I hope it will, we need more than just your rocket launching off into space. We need a fleet of rockets. We need a network marketing space fleet—one that can travel not just to the moon but to Mars, Jupiter, and beyond the solar system.

Imagine the lives such a mission could change.

That's my parting message to you. This isn't just about you. You should keep building your business not just because it makes you more money but because you're changing more lives.

And with any luck, soon we'll all meet among the stars.

CONCLUSION

I finish every speech with the same line: "I don't know if we're going with you or without you, but with network marketing, we are going to the moon!"

I've designed this book to try to ensure you're on board when we take off for the moon. I've tried to make the content as concise, fast-paced, and enjoyable as possible while including everything you need to know to build a successful network marketing business. But because I favored speed and accessibility, that necessarily meant I had to leave some things out.

For instance, I've tried to speak about the leadership role you'll need to take as you grow your business, but there's so much more to say, as indeed there is about putting together the best possible presentation or putting on a fantastic annual event.

You should see this book as a starting point. It can get you where you want to go. But a great network marketing business leader never stops learning or developing their business. Every entrepreneur knows there's always a better way to do things.

With that in mind, I recommend you continue your education even as you grow your business. I have more material for you on my website, www.sandrocazzato.com/moonshot, including PDF manuals, videos, and step-by-step guides that review and give more nuance to the process we've just covered. But that's just the beginning. I encourage you to immediately go read Eric Worre's *Go Pro* and Don Failla's *The 45-Second Presentation That Will Change Your Life*. Read Frazer Brookes's *I Dare Your* and learn how to develop your social media platform. And then keep reading! Read every resource you can on network marketing and business.

As I've said many times in this book, we aren't in the business of get-rich-quick. This is a business you can run for the rest of your career. Keep growing, keep learning—and enjoy your next walk out on the moon.

APPENDIX 1

ANSWERS TO TYPICAL QUESTIONS AND OBJECTIONS IN NETWORK MARKETING

I've included here eighteen of the most common objections and questions that come up when introducing someone to network marketing. Before you read, there are a couple things to keep in mind.

First, your answers should always be authentic and natural to you. Don't just memorize these and repeat them to everyone. Instead, take them as an example of the type of answer that works best. When the moment comes, phrase these answers in your own words, using your own experiences and the information you know about the person you're talking to.

Second, each objection includes two responses. The first is your follow-up question to gather that additional information from the person who has questions about network marketing.

You ask this to understand their unique concerns. The second response is an example answer. Again, be sure to use the information you gather from the follow-up and put it in your own words!

"ISN'T NETWORK MARKETING JUST A PYRAMID SCHEME?"

Follow-Up Question: "That's interesting. Can you explain to me quickly what you mean by pyramid scheme?"

Example Answer: "Most people confuse the two. A pyramid scheme is illegal and has no real product—only money changing hands. Network marketing has real products, real customers, and a system that rewards both sales and leadership. It's a legal and proven model, used by companies worldwide."

"I'M NOT GOOD AT SELLING."

Follow-Up Question: "What do you mean exactly by selling? How do you define it?"

Example Answer: "If by selling you mean pushing and convincing, then you don't need to be good at it—because that's not what we do. In network marketing, we share stories and experiences. If you can recommend a movie, a restaurant, or a product you like, you can do this. It's about connection, not pressure."

"MOST PEOPLE FAIL IN NETWORK MARKETING."

Follow-Up Question: "What does failure mean to you? How would you define it?"

Example Answer: "In reality, most people quit—and that's different from failing. It's like in any other business: most restaurants close in the first three years; most startups don't survive. Does that mean the business model doesn't work? No. It means people didn't commit long enough."

"I DON'T HAVE TIME."

Follow-Up Question: "What are you investing your time into right now that you'd never want to change?"

Example Answer: "Everybody has twenty-four hours. The question is about priorities. Most people start this business part-time, spending five to ten hours on it a week. You don't need to quit your job, you just need to redirect some time into something that can create freedom later."

"ISN'T THE MARKET ALREADY SATURATED?"

Follow-Up Question: "What do you mean by saturated? How would you recognize that?"

Example Answer: "Do you think people stopped opening gyms, restaurants, or fashion brands because 'there are too many?' Every year, new leaders rise, new products launch, and new markets open. The only saturation is in people's imagination. Opportunity never goes out of style."

"DO I NEED TO KNOW A LOT OF PEOPLE?"

Follow-Up Question: "How many people would you say you know in total—even just casually?"

Example Answer: "Most people underestimate their network. But even if you start from zero, this business is designed to expand your world. With social media, events, and teamwork, your circle will grow naturally. You'll be surprised how many people you'll meet along the way."

"I DON'T WANT TO BOTHER MY FRIENDS AND FAMILY."

Follow-Up Question: "What does bother mean to you? What would that look like?"

Example Answer: "This business isn't about pushing. It's about offering value and solutions. If you believe in what you share, you're giving people a chance. Your friends and family are not your final market anyway. Your long-term success comes from building real leadership and community."

"ISN'T THIS RISKY?"

Follow-Up Question: "Compared to what? What do you see as safe?"

Example Answer: "Every path has risk. But compared to starting a restaurant, a franchise, or a startup, this risk is tiny. No massive investments, no employees, no rent. The bigger risk is staying where you are, with no chance of change."

"WHAT IF PEOPLE LAUGH AT ME?"

Follow-Up Question: "Has it ever happened that someone laughed at an idea you had and it later worked out?"

Example Answer: "People always laugh at pioneers. They laughed at the founders of Amazon, Uber, and Airbnb. They laugh until you succeed—then they ask how you did it. If you live for other people's opinions, you'll always stay small."

"HOW LONG UNTIL I MAKE MONEY?"

Follow-Up Question: "How fast do you usually expect to see results when you start something new?"

Example Answer: "This is a business, not a lottery. Some people earn in the first month; others take longer. It depends on your effort, focus, and willingness to learn. But the key is this: you're building something that can last, not just earn you a quick payday."

"I'VE HEARD ONLY THE PEOPLE AT THE TOP MAKE MONEY."

Follow-Up Question: "What do you mean by top? How do you think people get there?"

Example Answer: "In network marketing, everyone starts at the bottom. There's no shortcut. The so-called 'top' worked their way up through consistency and leadership. Every year, new people climb ranks. The plan is built so that anyone who performs can succeed."

"I DON'T LIKE RECRUITING."

Follow-Up Question: "What do you mean exactly by recruiting?"

Example Answer: "If you mean chasing people and trying to convince them to join you, I agree—that's not fun. But real recruiting is about inviting, sharing, and showing an option. It's not about hunting people; it's about being visible enough that the right people find you."

"I'M NOT A LEADER."

Follow-Up Question: "What's your definition of leadership?"

Example Answer: "Leadership is not a title; it's a choice. Nobody is born a leader. They grow into it. This business is a leadership development program with a compensation plan attached. Step by step, you'll learn to lead yourself and then others."

"ISN'T THIS TOO GOOD TO BE TRUE?"

Follow-Up Question: "What part seems too good to you?"

Example Answer: "The model is disruptive, yes—and that's why people doubt it. But it's built on simple logic: instead of paying millions to advertising agencies, companies pay real people to distribute and share. It's not 'too good'; it's just a smarter way."

"WHAT IF I GET REJECTED?"

Follow-Up Question: "How do you usually handle rejection in life?"

Example Answer: "Rejection is part of every business. It's never about you. It's about timing, priorities, or the other person's mindset. Every 'no' brings you closer to a 'yes.' In fact, rejection is your tuition fee in entrepreneurship."

"I DON'T WANT TO PRESSURE PEOPLE."

Follow-Up Question: "What do you mean by pressure?"

Example Answer: "Pressure means convincing someone against their will. That's not what professionals do. We share, we invite, and we show by example. People follow inspiration, not pressure."

"WHAT IF I'M NOT SUCCESSFUL?"

Follow-Up Question: "What would success mean to you in this context?"

Example Answer: "Success is never guaranteed in any business. But here's what's guaranteed: you'll grow as a person, learn new skills, meet new people, and open new doors. The person you become is already a winner. And often, financial success follows naturally."

"IS THIS REALLY PROFESSIONAL?"

Follow-Up Question: "What do you mean by professional?"

Example Answer: "There are amateurs in every industry—and unfortunately, network marketing has many. But done right, this is one of the most professional, scalable business models today. It's entrepreneurship with leadership at the core."

ACKNOWLEDGMENTS

One of the most wonderful aspects of network marketing is the fact each of us is an independent entrepreneur seeking to fulfill our own goals and dreams, and yet, we can't achieve that without working together. It's a team of individuals—and that is our strength. It's what allows us to shoot for the moon and beyond.

In the same way, this book is not just the result of my own experience and effort; it would be impossible without my team. Leaders like Marijana Markovic, Neuza Calado, Manuela Selimovic, Edita Dzehverovic, and Alessandro Vegliante have been a constant source of ideas and inspiration from the beginning. Others like Mikey Willemart, Funda Kalkan, Manuela Buchner, Celia Terrones, Yann Werle, Stephanie Terrones, Vincenzo Amatulli, Julia Baylan, Jiri Sedek, Irina Ayari, Alexandra Baidoc, and Francesco Picciotto have shown me just how powerful the concepts we've covered in the book truly are.

Everything I've achieved is only possible because of their effort, their skill, and their belief in me.

I also want to reserve a special thank you for Michelangelo Paradiso for the trust you placed in me.

At the same time, I could never have learned all that I know about network marketing without the mentorship of three of the most brilliant minds in the industry: Eric Worre, Frazer Brookes, and Denis Gava. This book exists because I am standing on the shoulders of these giants.

And then there is my great friend Samuel: the person who has continued to push me to finally put together this book. He's supported me throughout the entire process. I couldn't have done this without you.

To end, I want to thank my wife, my kids, my parents, and my brother. You're what makes it all worthwhile. Thank you for letting me go on this journey to fulfillment. I love you.

ABOUT THE AUTHOR

Born in Switzerland with Italian roots, **SANDRO CAZZATO** built his first career in IT and finance before discovering his true calling in Network Marketing. Today, he is among the most successful leaders in the world, guiding an organization of over 170,000 people across countries and cultures. As the founder of the Essence Tribe community, he combines entrepreneurship, leadership, and heart to help others unlock their potential and design the life they dream of.

His story is proof that with vision, courage, and commitment, success is not a matter of luck—it's a matter of design.